Sampler Book 12, Ontario in Colour Photos, Saving Our History One Photo at a Time

Photography by Barbara Raué
©2019

Series Name: Sampler Cruising Ontario

Sampling from Haldimand County

Each photo I take that precedes a demolition, or a natural disaster such as a tornado or a fire, is meeting this aim of mine of Saving Our History One Photo at a Time. There are more than 100 towns already photographed which you can visit without moving from a comfortable chair in your living room.

©All the photos in this book have been taken with my cameras. I own the rights to them.

Cover: 601 Haldimand Road 12, Fisherville, Page 21

Table of Contents

Caledonia, Ontario – My Top 6 Picks

Hagersville, Ontario – My Top 6 Picks

Jarvis, Ontario – My Top 6 Picks

Fisherville, Nanticoke, Selkirk, Ontario in Colour Photos – My Top 16 Picks

Cayuga and York, Ontario in Colour Photos – My Top 14 Picks

Dunnville, Ontario Book 1 in Colour Photos – My Top 11 Picks

Dunnville, Ontario Book 2 and Area in Colour Photos – My Top 16 Picks

Caledonia, Ontario – My Top 6 Picks

Caledonia is a small riverside community located on the Grand River in Haldimand County. It is located at the intersection of Highway 6 and Highway 54 (within the town, these streets are called Argyle Street and Caithness Street respectively). On Highway 6, the town is 10 kilometers south of Hamilton and 10 kilometers north of Hagersville. On Highway 54, the town is 15 kilometers east of Brantford and 10 kilometers west of Cayuga.

The Grand River flows 293 kilometers from the Dundalk Highlands to Lake Erie and is the largest river in southern Ontario. The river winds its way through marshes, woods, farmsteads, and communities. Rainbow trout use this river in their migration.

Caledonia was once a small strip of land between Seneca and Oneida villages. The Grand River traveled through Caledonia dividing it into two sides, North and South. In 1834, Ranald McKinnon was hired to build a dam in Seneca and a dam in Caledonia. Completed in 1840, the dams made water power available. The dam at Caledonia was constructed as part of a series of dams, locks and canals to facilitate navigation of the Grand River from Lake Erie to Brantford. Mills were built throughout Seneca village, and five mills were built in Caledonia by 1850. Commercial navigation ceased by 1879, but the dam continued to serve the local mills and provided a recreation opportunity. The present dam was built in 1980 downstream of the original structure.

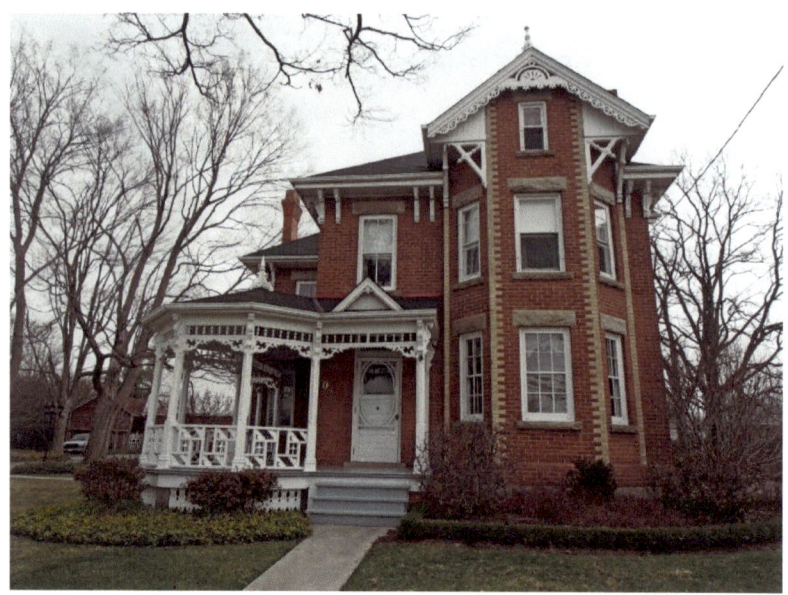

204 Caithness Street – paired cornice brackets, corner quoins, decorative verge board trim on gable of two-and-a-half-storey tower-like bay

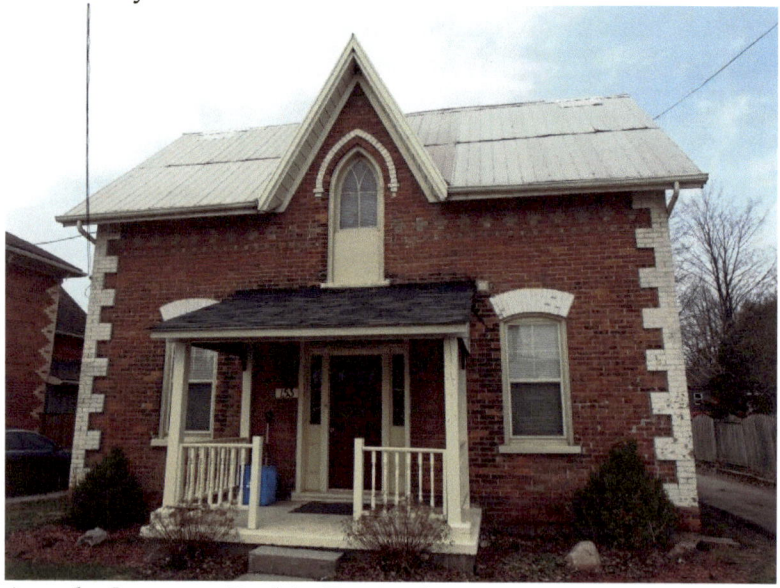

153 Argyle Street – Gothic Revival cottage, corner quoins, decorative brickwork

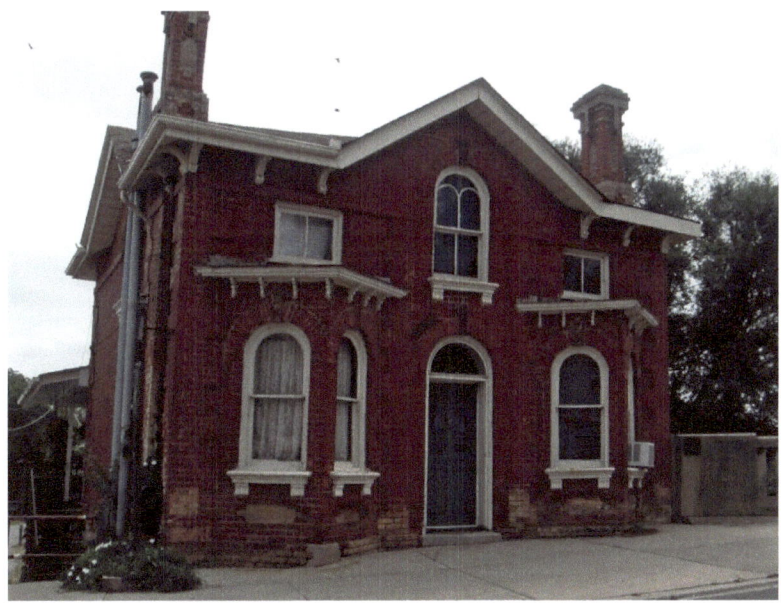

4 Argyle Street – Toll House c. 1875 – built as an office and residence for the collector of tolls for the bridge over the Grand River

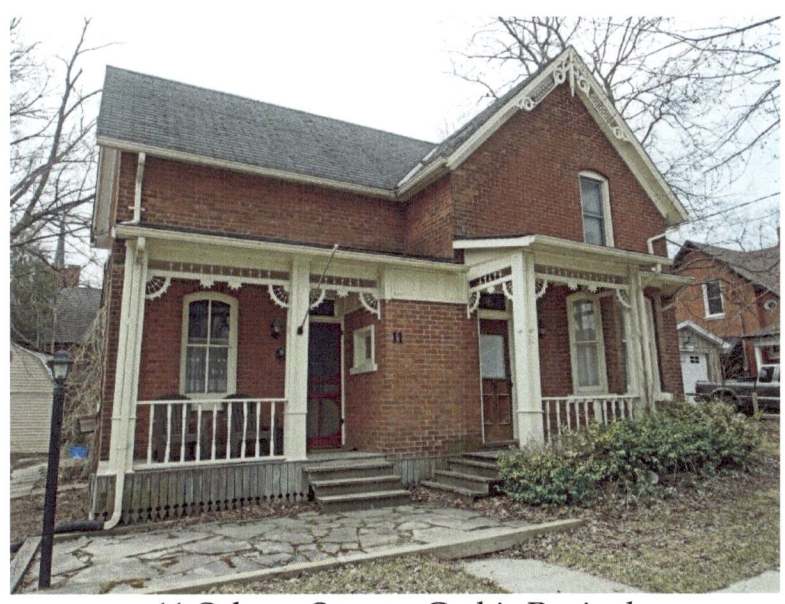

11 Orkney Street – Gothic Revival

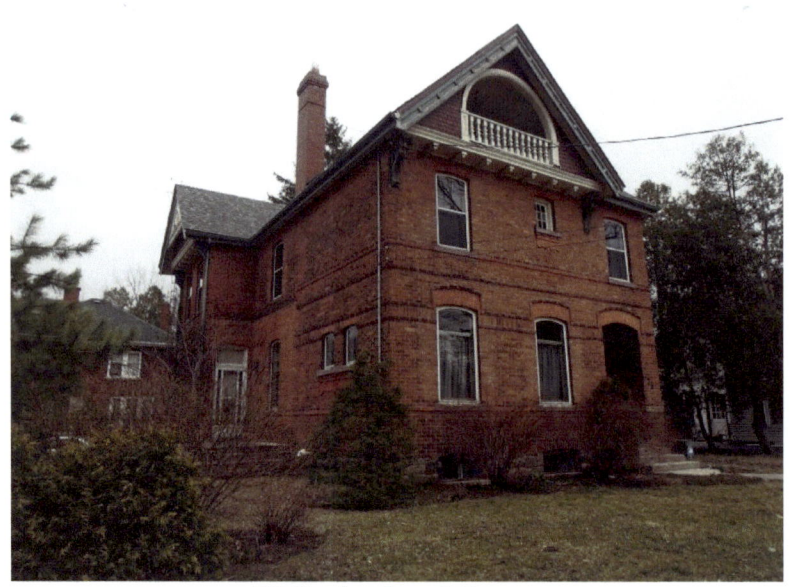

78 Sutherland Street

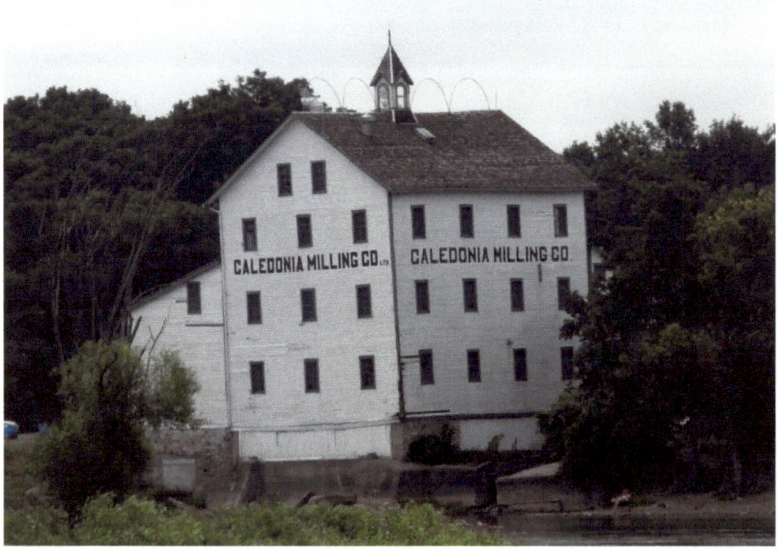

Grand River Mills – Caledonia Milling Co. – built in 1846 - the last timber-frame water powered mill along the Grand River in Ontario

Hagersville, Ontario – My Top 6 Picks

Hagersville, a community in Haldimand County, is located about 45 kilometers southwest of Hamilton, Ontario, and 15 kilometers southwest of Caledonia.

In 1852, Charles Hager built a frame hotel at the corner of the Plank Road and Indian Line. It was called The Junction Hotel and later The Lawson Hotel after a change in ownership. Hagersville's first post office was in this hotel. With the construction of the Plank Road, a small village popped up in 1855 when Charles and David Hager bought most of the land in the center of the area. David Almas owned the land on the east side of the road, while John Porter owned the land in the west end. Joseph Seymour suggested the community be called Hagersville to honor the Hager brothers.

The building of the Canada Southern Railroad in 1870, and of the Hamilton and Lake Erie Railway three years later helped to make Hagersville a prosperous village.

Hagersville gained notoriety in 1990 with a huge uncontrolled tire fire which spewed toxic smoke into the atmosphere for seventeen days. The fire actually occurred in Townsend, a neighboring community, but media labeled it as Hagersville due to Townsend's relatively unknown status in the area.

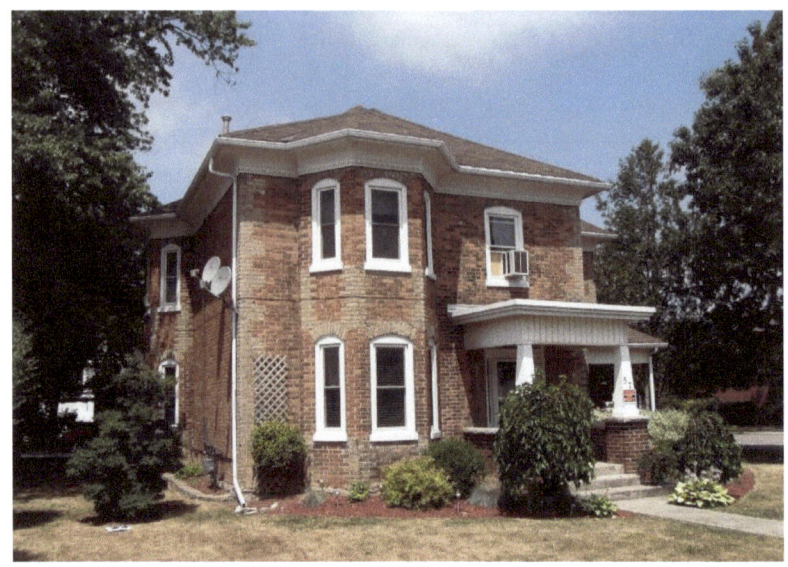

Italianate style, dichromatic brickwork, two-storey bay window

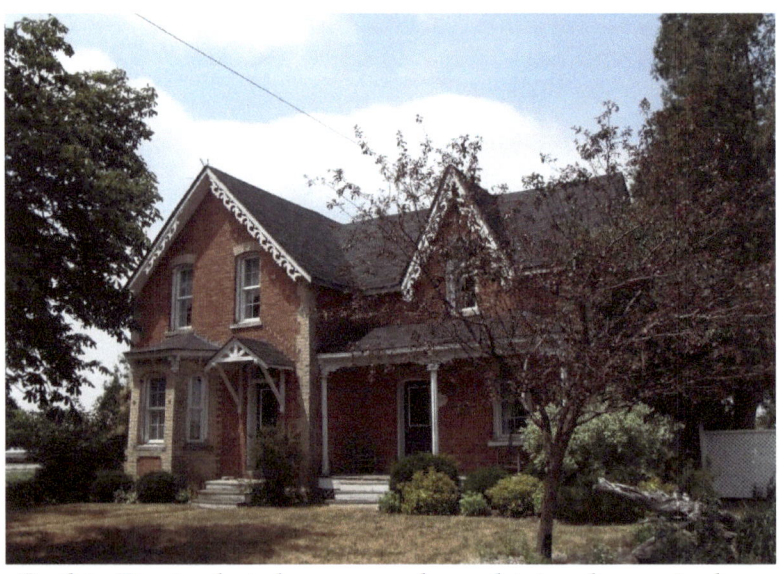

Gothic Revival style – verge board trim, bay window

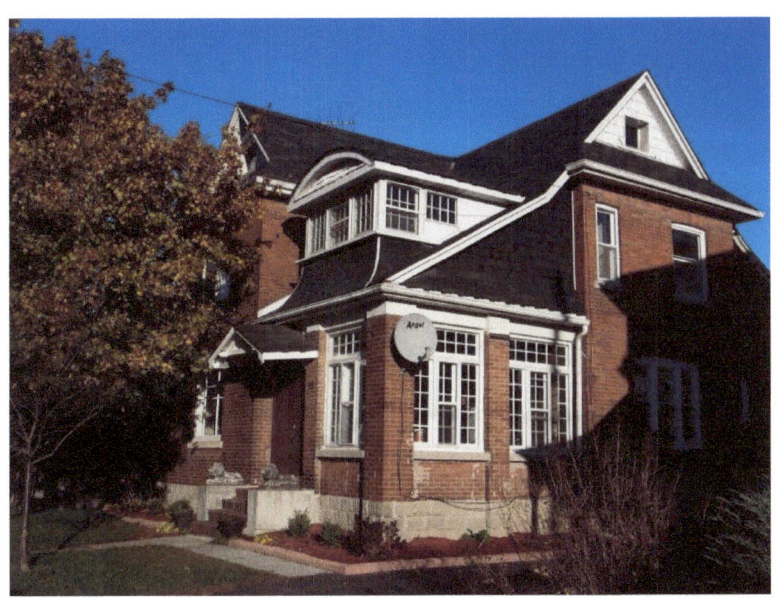

Queen Anne style

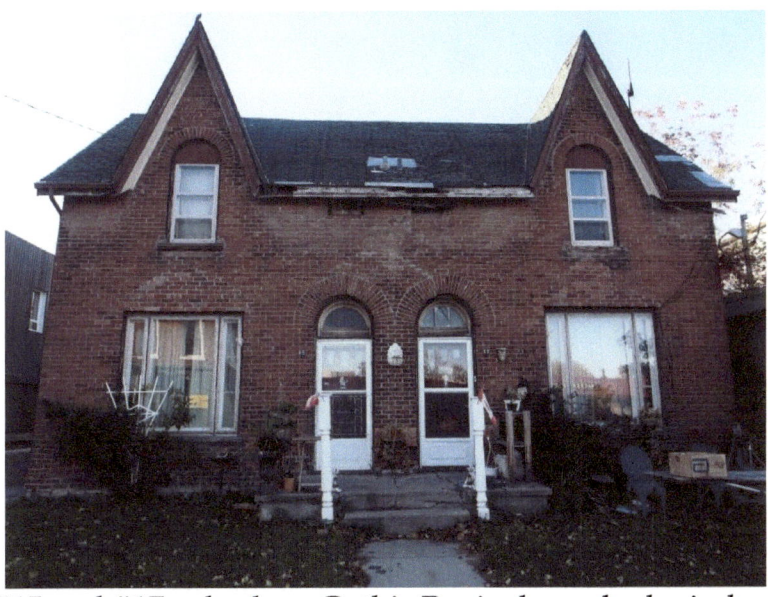

#15 and #17 – duplex - Gothic Revival – arched window voussoirs

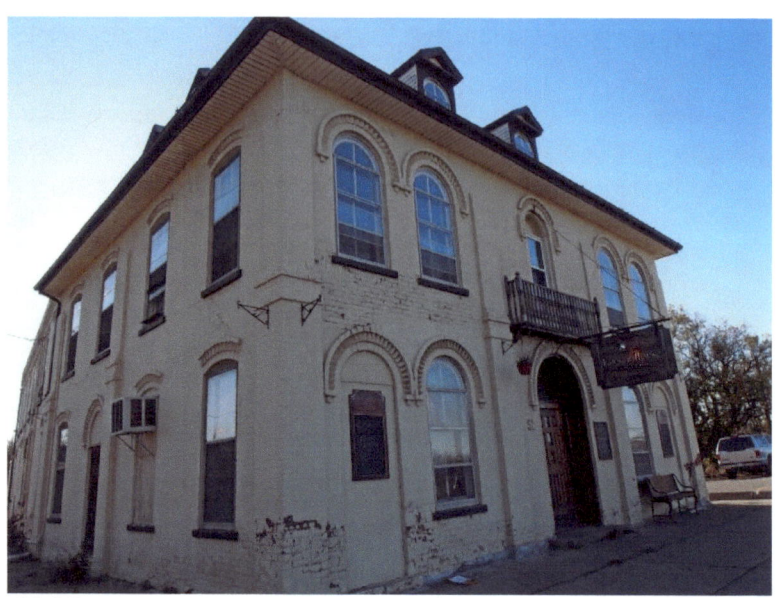

The Old Lawson House Eatery and Pub – dormers, Italianate style, arched window voussoirs

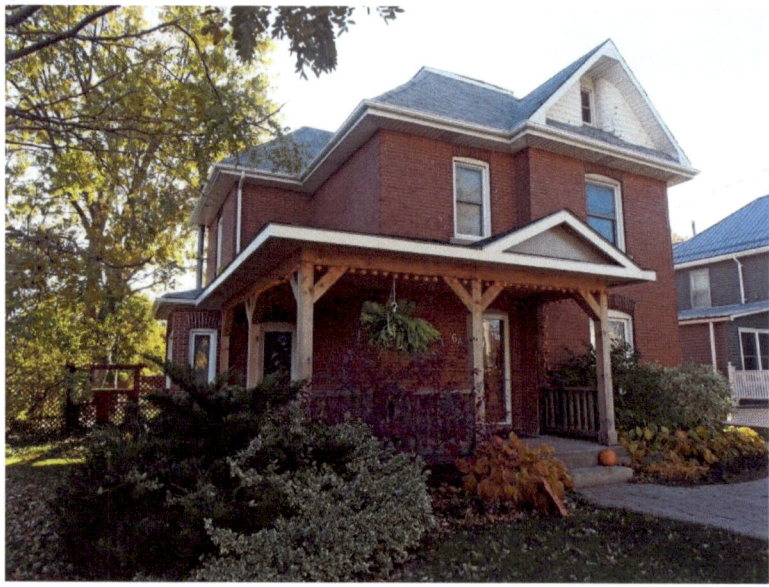

#64 - Edwardian/Italianate style

Jarvis, Ontario – My Top 6 Picks

Jarvis is located in Haldimand County near the towns of Simcoe, Cayuga, Port Dover and Hagersville. Jarvis is strategically located at the junction of Highways 3 and 6. Jarvis has some excellent examples of brick architecture. Many of the historic homes were built after 1873. Many of the town's restaurants and shops are clustered around the intersection of the highways. The majority of the buildings are red brick.

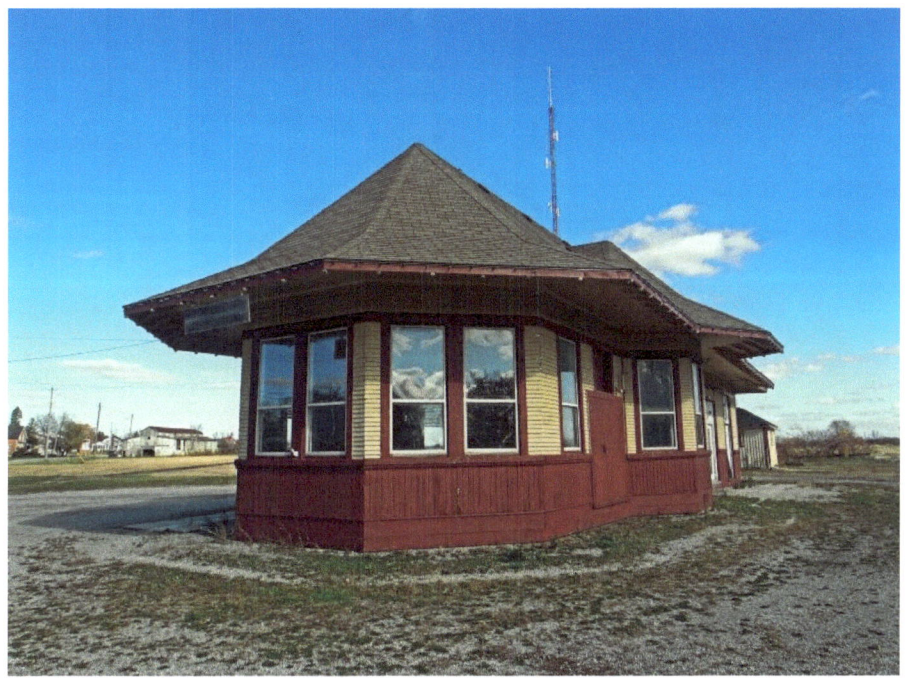

Jarvis Train Station

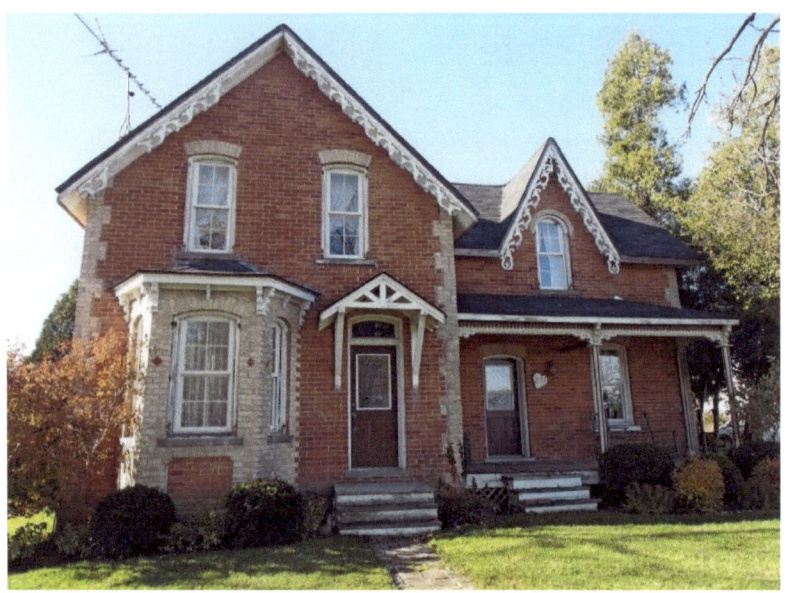

2145 Main Street - Gothic Revival – verge board trim, bay window with cornice brackets

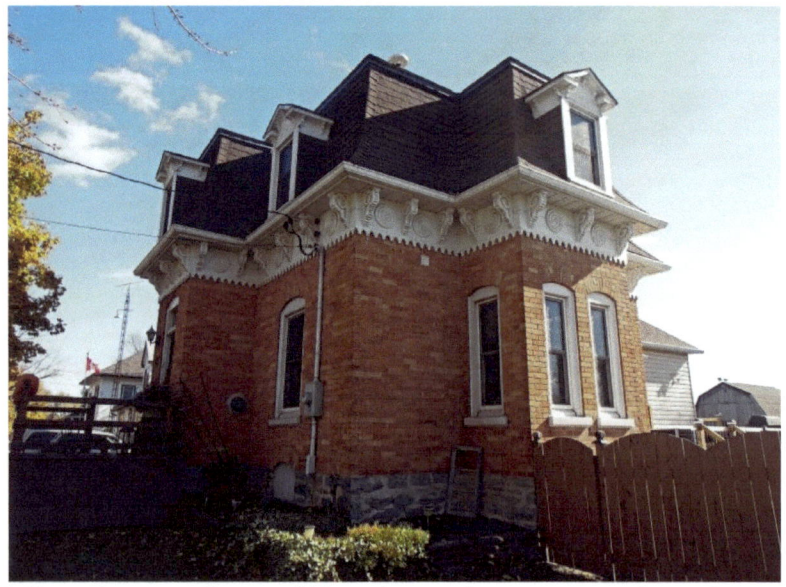

45 Talbot Street – Second Empire style – mansard roof, dormers in roof, single cornice brackets, cornice return on small gables on window dormers

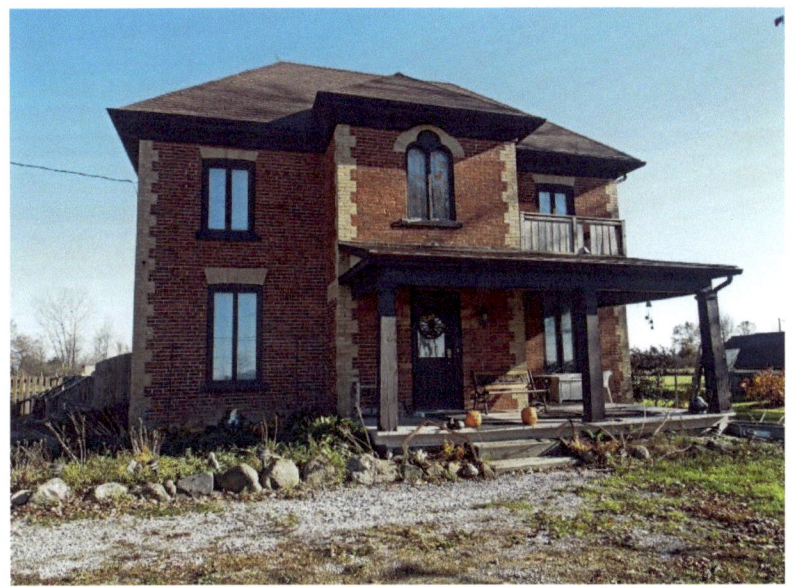

c. 1847 – Italianate, hipped roof, dichromatic brickwork

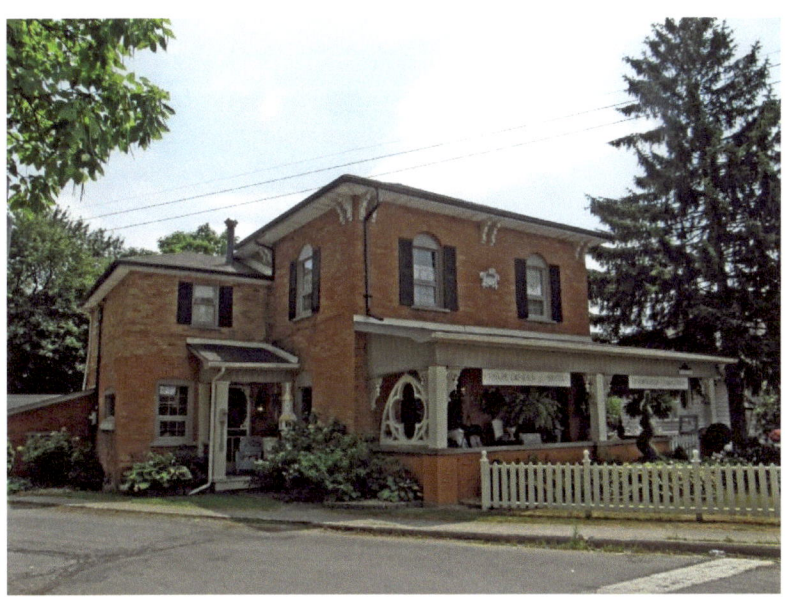

2092 Main Street – Italianate – c. 1870 - Italianate style

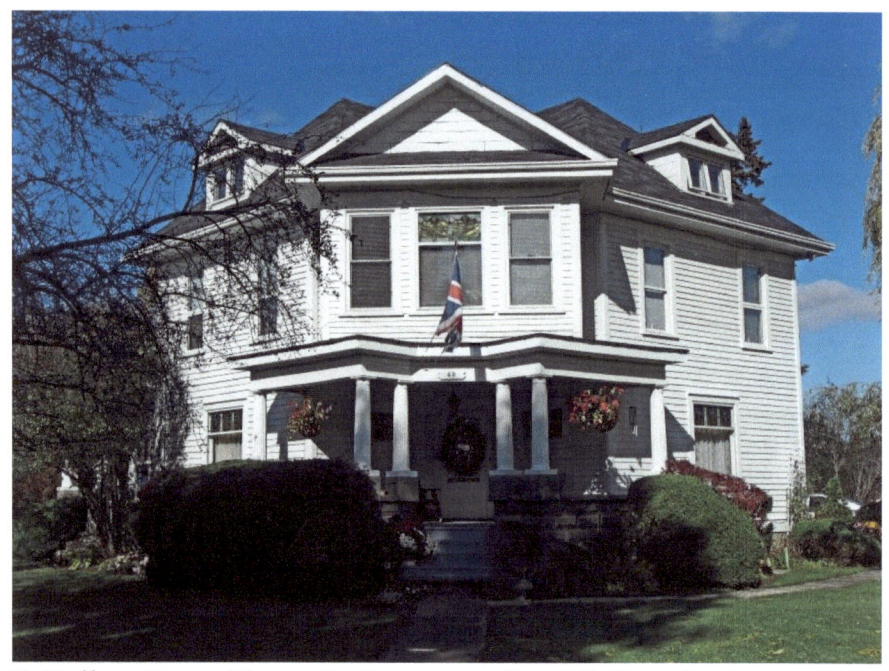

60 Talbot Street East – Italianate style with frontispiece, triangular pediment, dormers in the attic

Fisherville, Nanticoke, Selkirk, Ontario in Colour Photos – My Top 16 Picks

Haldimand County is a municipality on the Niagara Peninsula in Southern Ontario, on the north shore of Lake Erie, and on the Grand River. Haldimand was first created as a county in 1800, from a portion of Norfolk. It was named after the governor of the Province of Quebec Sir Frederick Haldimand. From 1974 to 2000, Haldimand County and Norfolk County were merged to form the Regional Municipality of Haldimand-Norfolk.

The population centers in Haldimand are Caledonia, Dunnville, Hagersville, Jarvis and Cayuga. Most of Haldimand is agricultural land, although some heavy industry, including the Nanticoke Generating Station, is located here. Some of the smaller communities within the municipality are Byng, Canborough, Canfield, Cheapside, Fisherville, Kohler, Lowbanks, Nanticoke, Rainham Centre, Selkirk, South Cayuga, Sweets Corners, and York.

Township of Rainham

The first white inhabitants of Rainham were Jacob Hoover with his sons Abraham, David, Benjamin and Daniel who came from Pennsylvania in 1791, traveling in wagons in which they carried all their moveable possessions.

They purchased about 2,500 acres of land from the government. The Hoovers were Mennonites of Swiss descent. The Hoovers were a thrifty and industrious family and soon had large clearings. They became wealthy as they were the first settlers who had any surplus produce to sell to others who came a few years later.

Manufactured items were very expensive so the settlers made as many items as they could. Many of them made their own harness of basswood bark boiled in lye which was a fair substitute for leather.

The township covers about 25,000 acres with stiff clay soil that is very productive and well cultivated. Fisherville and Rainham Centre are the only villages wholly in the township. Fisherville is the center of the German settlement and has a population of about one hundred and fifty people.

Nanticoke

Nanticoke is located on the western border of Haldimand County. Nanticoke is located directly across Lake Erie from the United States city of Erie, Pennsylvania. Unlike the majority of Haldimand or Norfolk County, Nanticoke is a highly industrialized community. This community is southeast of Simcoe in neighboring Norfolk County and south of Brantford. Nanticoke's residential area is bordered on the west by the Nanticoke Industrial Park, home to the U.S. Steel Canada Lake Erie Works and a number of smaller businesses.

The Esso Refinery Nanticoke is on the northeast, and the Nanticoke Generating Station is on the southeast. Nanticoke used to be a bustling farming and fishing community inhabited since the late eighteenth century. Nanticoke adapted to the Industrial Revolution and became a desired spot for heavy industry.

In 1974, Nanticoke was incorporated as a city within the Regional Municipality of Haldimand-Norfolk through the amalgamation of the towns of Port Dover and Waterford, the village of Jarvis, and parts of the townships of Rainham, Townsend, Walpole and Woodhouse. In 2001, the town and all other municipalities within the region were dissolved and the region was divided into two single tier municipalities with city-status but called counties. What was the city of Nanticoke is now split between Haldimand County and Norfolk County. Wind Turbines were installed in November 2013.

Cheapside

Cheapside is located in the Regional Municipality of Haldimand-Norfolk and is part of the City of Nanticoke. I n 1854 David Silverthom settled here and opened the first store. He was bought out in 1860 by William Pugsley who called the place Cheap Corner. When the post office opened around 1865 the postal department proposed the present name which was accepted by residents.

Selkirk

Lake Erie shoreline, quiet roads and countryside make Selkirk a haven for travelers. Selkirk is located forty-five kilometers southwest of Hamilton and a short drive from Dunnville, Cayuga, Port Dover and Simcoe. Selkirk is the oldest village in Walpole Township. Settled by the Hoover family around 1800, the village was the site of a mill and an important center for the local farming community. When the post office opened in 1831 the village was called Walpole. In 1855, the village was renamed Selkirk, in honor of Thomas Douglas, Lord Selkirk, who once owned land in the area.

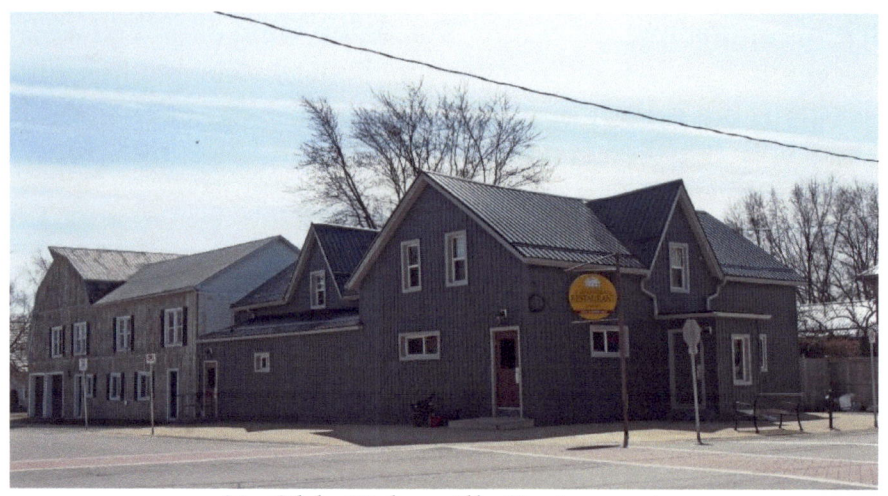
Ye Olde Fisherville Restaurant

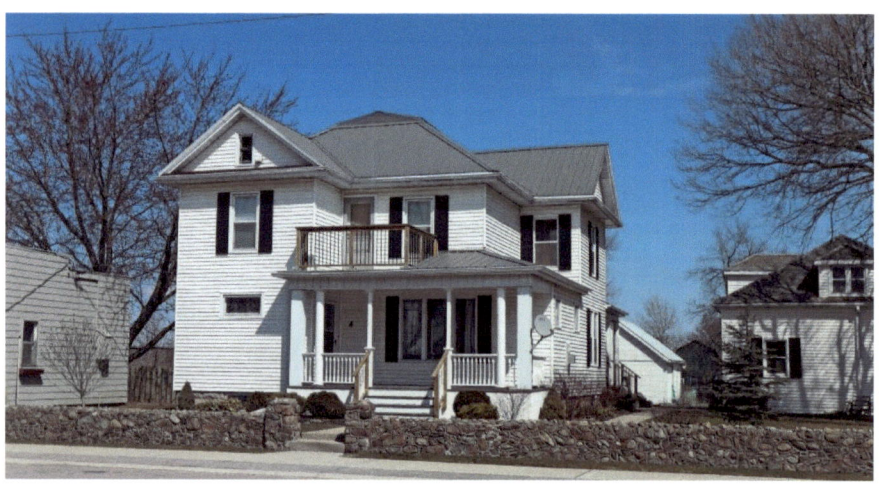
#4 – second floor balcony

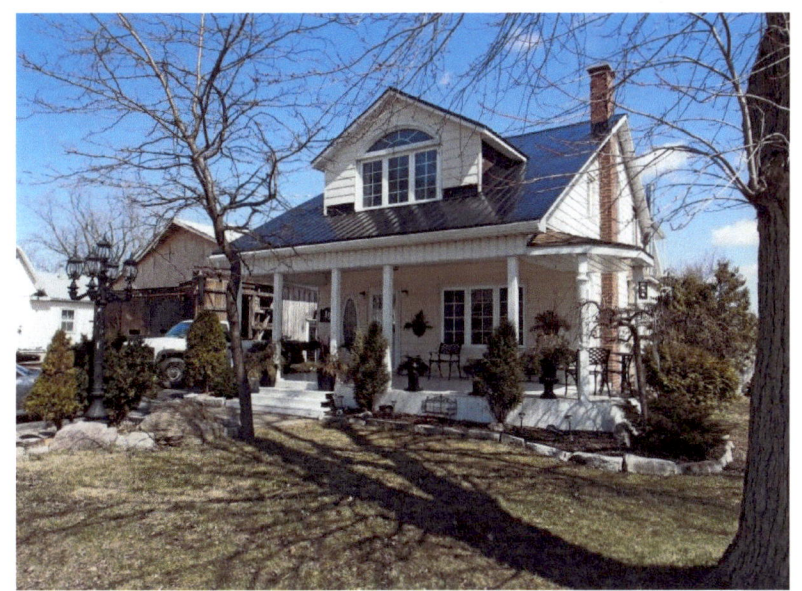

#19 – larger dormer, wraparound veranda

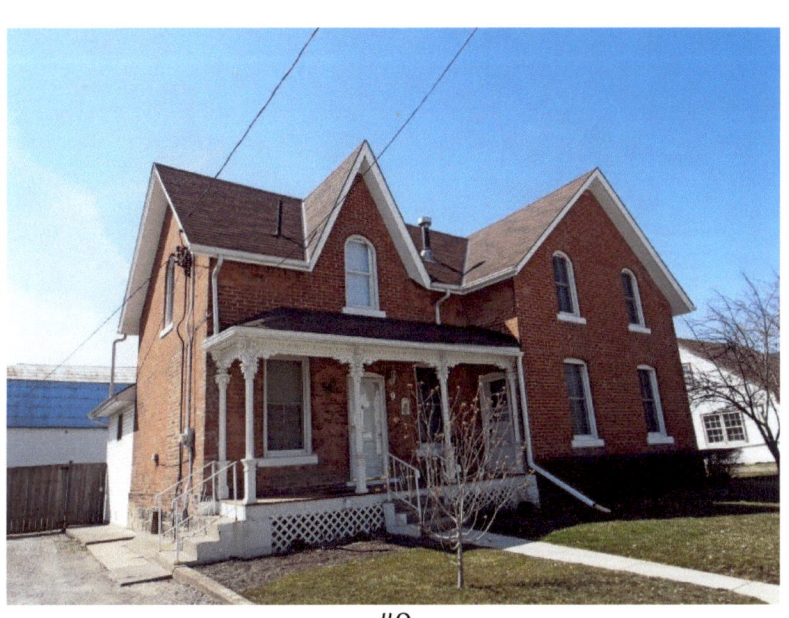

#9

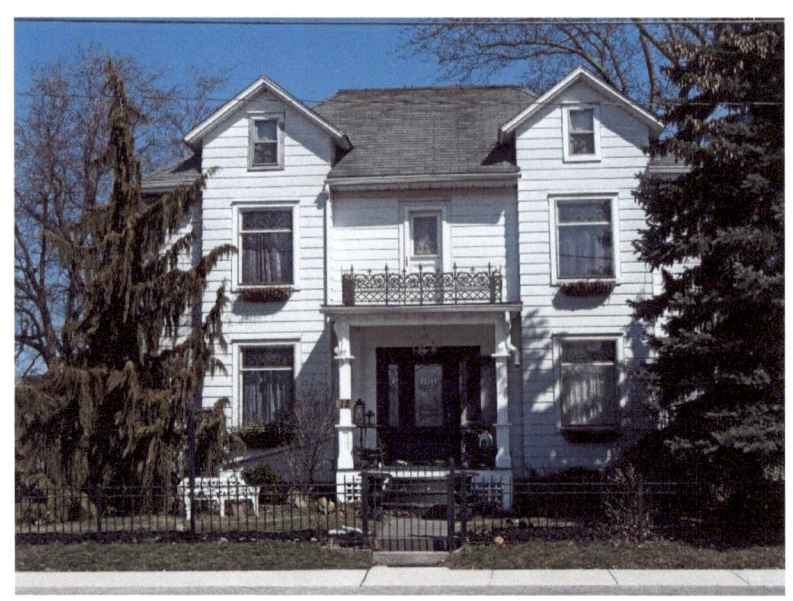

#12

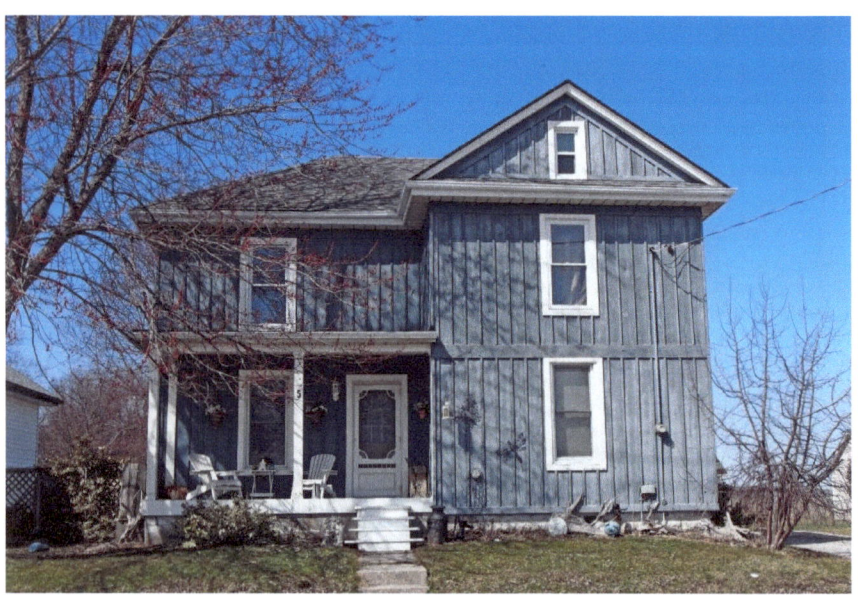

#5

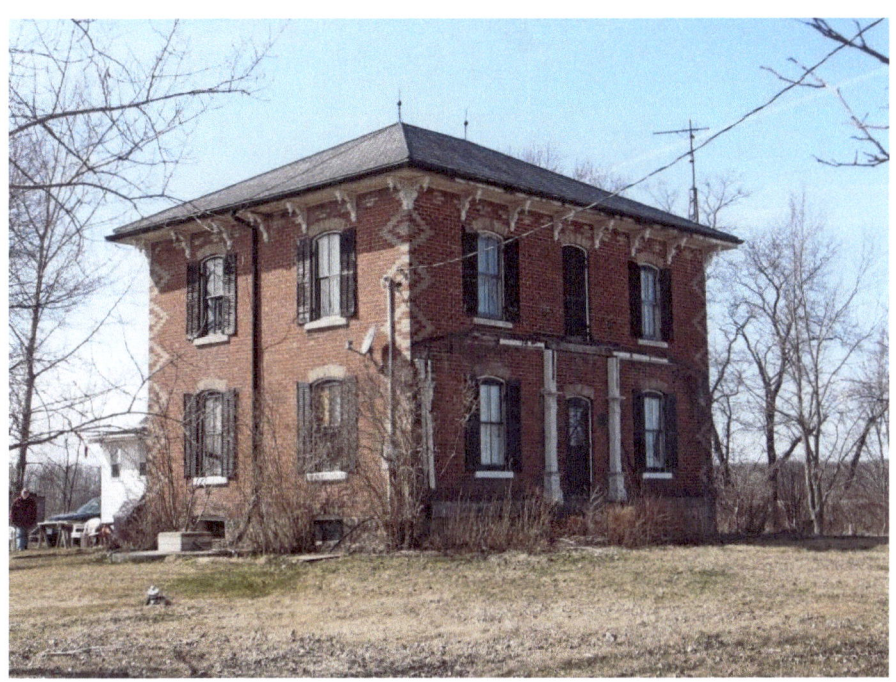

601 Haldimand Road 12 – The Charles Reicheld House crafted by traditional German carpenter Valentine Hartwick in 1886 – farmhouse with cornice brackets, dichromatic brickwork, hipped roof

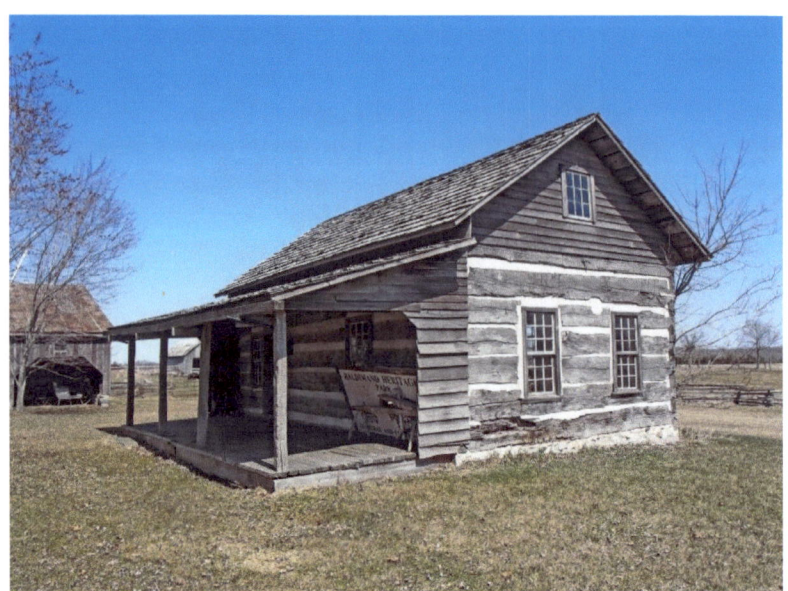

95 Concession 4 – The Hoover log house built in 1793 on the Lake Erie shore south of Selkirk for Daniel Hoover, son of Jacob Hoover from Pennsylvania. In 1997, the fire damaged remnants were brought by Mr. Bill Fletcher, reassembled and relocated on his farm.

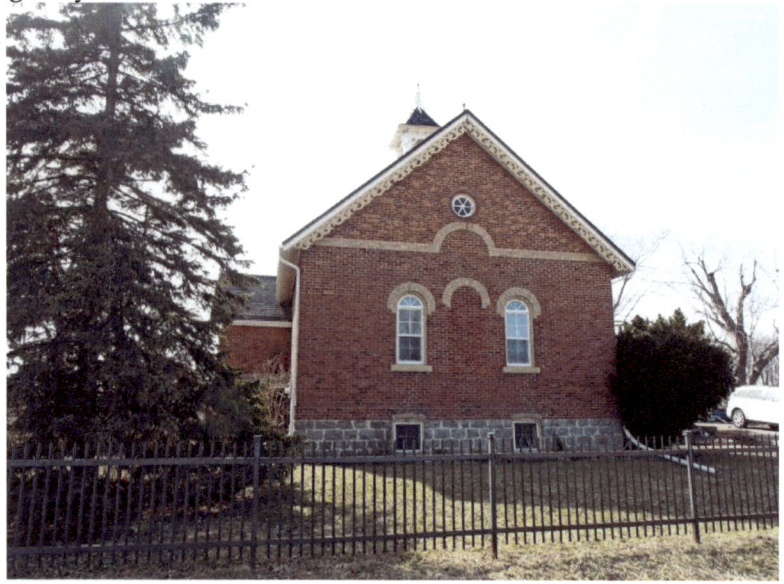

255 Kohler Road, Rainham Centre

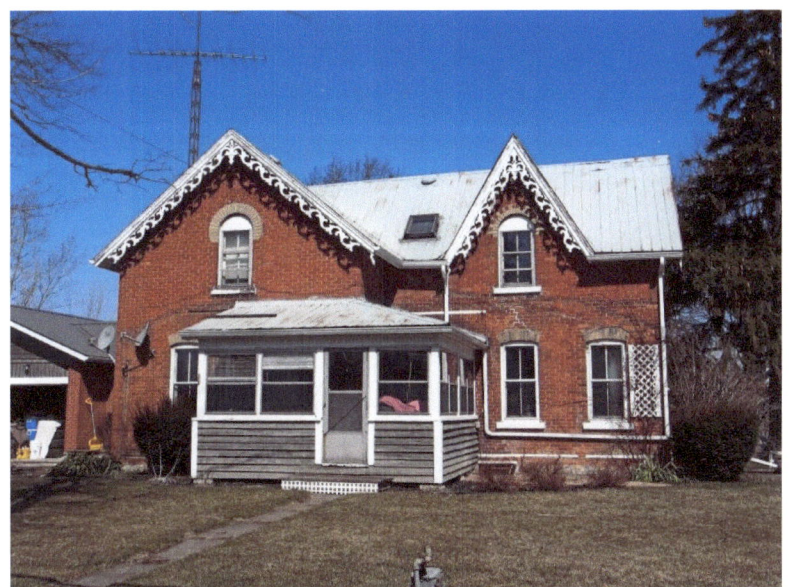

Gothic Revival – verge board trim on gables, Nanticoke

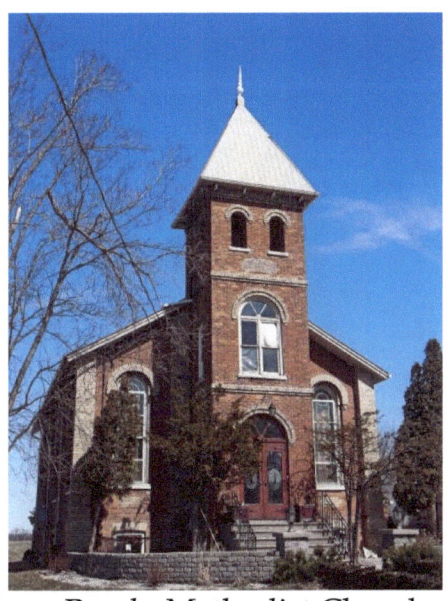

Rainham Road - Methodist Church – 1874

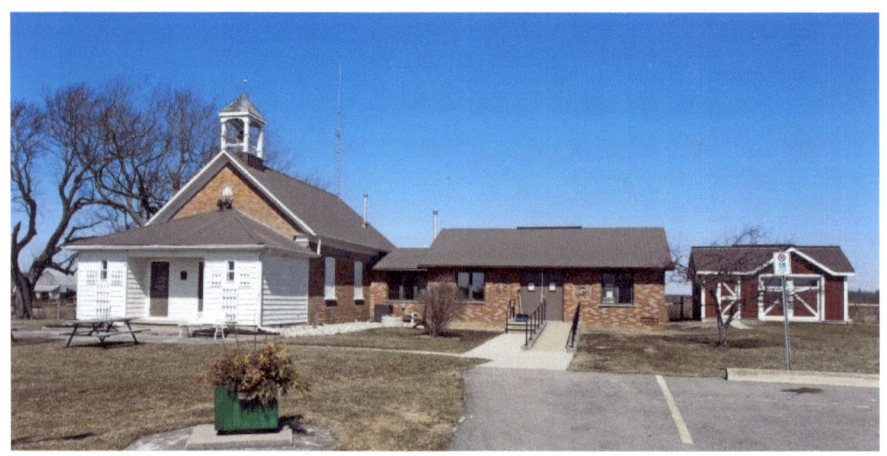

Wilson MacDonald Memorial School Museum, Cheapside – The original square framed school was opened on land owned by James Buckley and was replaced by this red brick one in 1872. It closed in 1965 and reopened in 1967 as a museum and memorial to Wilson MacDonald, a former student and renowned poet.

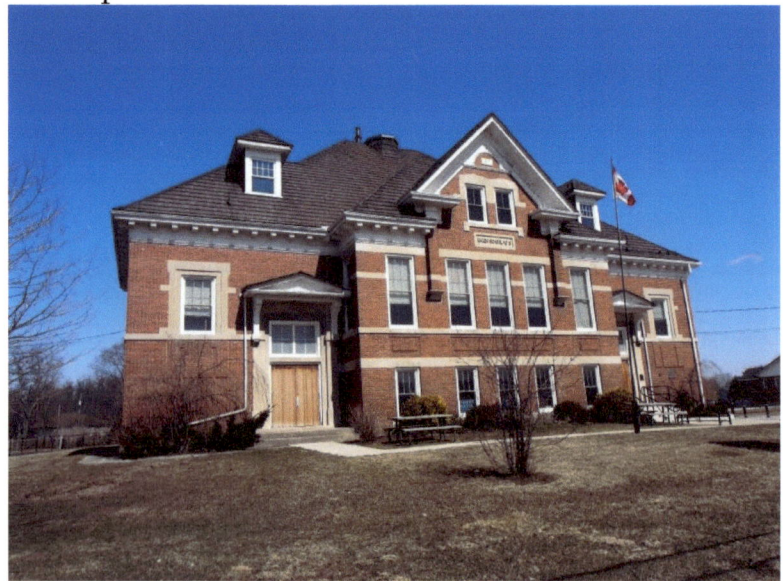

S.S. No. 3 Union School, Selkirk – 1918 – the school closed in 1949. It reopened in 1967 as a library and Selkirk Centennial Community Centre.

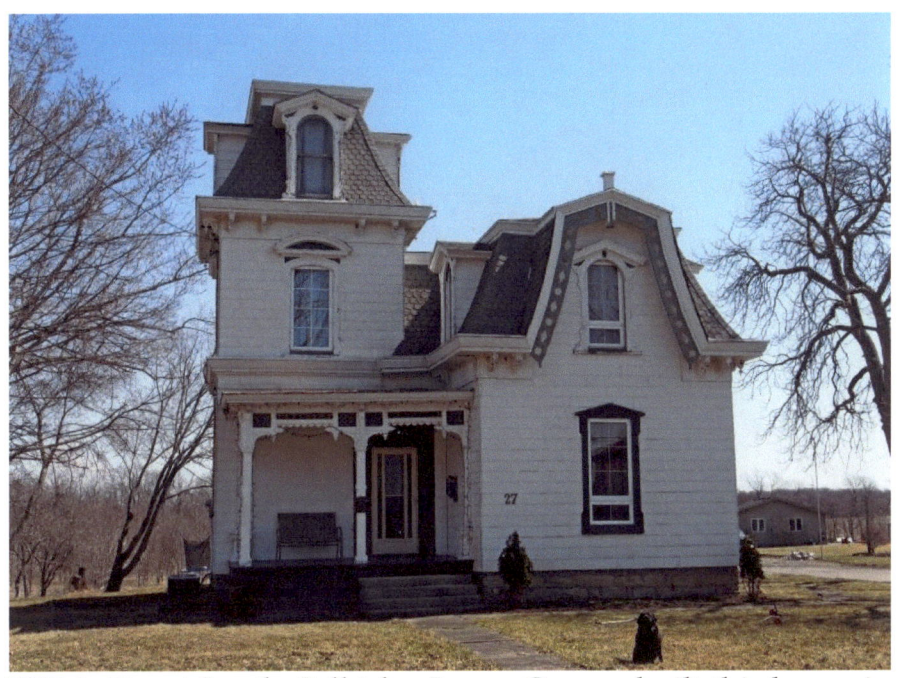

27 Erie Street South, Selkirk – James Cooper built this house in 1870. In 1878 he sold it to George Hoover. The frame house has irregular massing and is in the Second Empire style. It has an over-sized horseshoe dormer with bargeboard and finial, elaborate window molds with pediments. The three-storey tower has four dormers in the mansard roof. The Fess family purchased it in 1947.

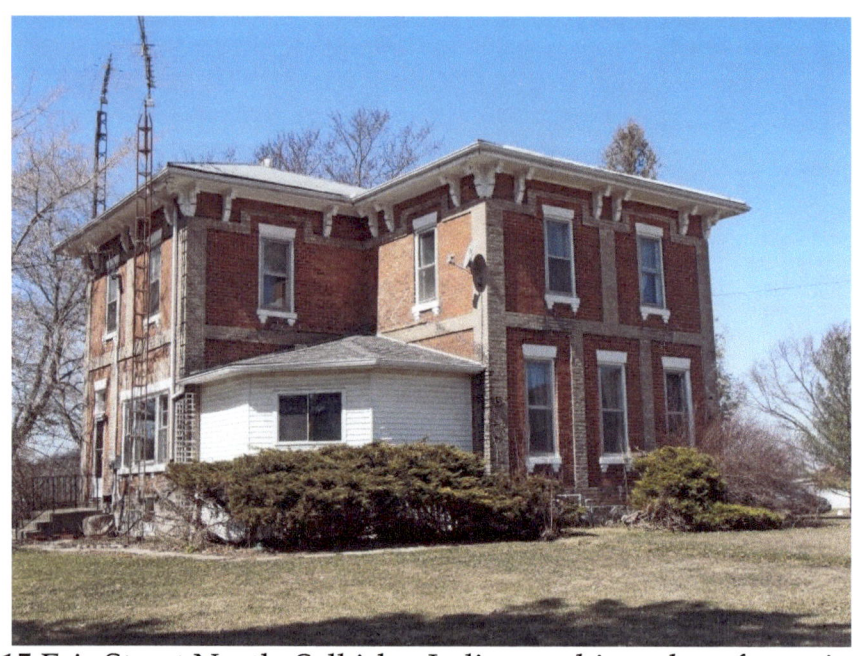

15 Erie Street North, Selkirk – Italianate, hipped roof, cornice brackets, quoins, banding

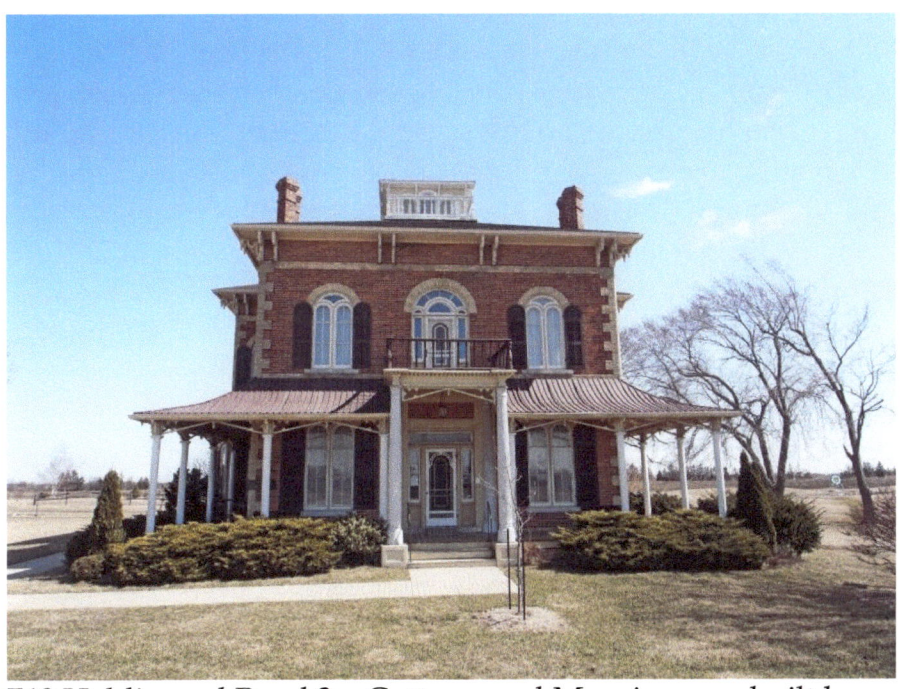

740 Haldimand Road 3 – Cottonwood Mansion was built by William Holmes circa 1860 in the Italianate architectural style. It is a 6,000 square foot home building. It has sixteen rooms, including five bedrooms, a music room and a widow's walk and rooftop belvedere. Corner quoins, bay window, paired cornice brackets

Cayuga and York, Ontario in Colour Photos – My Top 14 Picks

Early patterns of settlement in Haldimand County are still visible in the landscape and architecture, spanning from the pre-Contact era to the proclamation of the Haldimand Land Grant for the Six Nations and the subsequent migration of Loyalist settlers – Americans, largely of German descent and Mennonite tradition. Throughout the 1800s, immigration from the British Isles contributed significantly to the area's development, as did the small but industrious Black community of the late nineteenth century – many descended from ex-slaves of the American South. Since the post-war years of the twentieth century, a significant stream of immigration from the Netherlands has also added to our ever-expanding mosaic of cultural identity, as have the age-old traditions of our Indigenous neighbors – the Six Nations and New Credit communities.

Following the American Revolution, Sir Frederick Haldimand, Governor-in-Chief of Canada, granted in 1784 to the Six Nations of the Iroquois a tract of land extending for six miles on both sides of the Grand River from its source to Lake Erie. This grant was made in recognition of their services as allies of the British Crown during the war, and to recompense them for the loss of their former lands in northern New York State. In later years, large areas of this tract, including portions of the present counties of Haldimand, Brant, Waterloo and Wellington, were sold to white settlers. By 1853, Cayuga had lumber yards, a foundry, and a glass factory.

At its height, York had twenty businesses that included mills, inns, shoemakers, general stores, blacksmiths, and a lumber yard. It had a two-room school house and two churches.

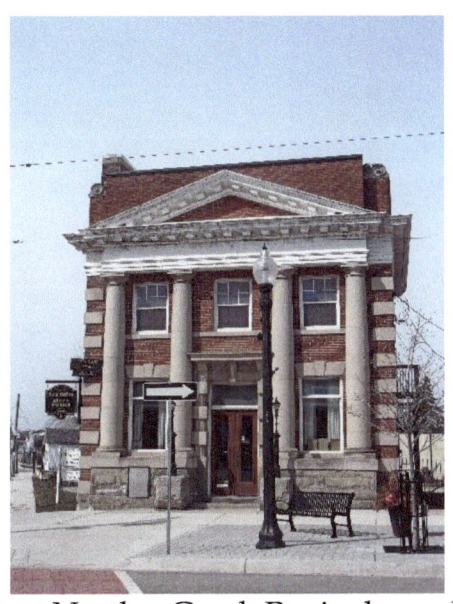

1 Cayuga Street North – Greek Revival – pediment above Doric pillars, keystones, quoins

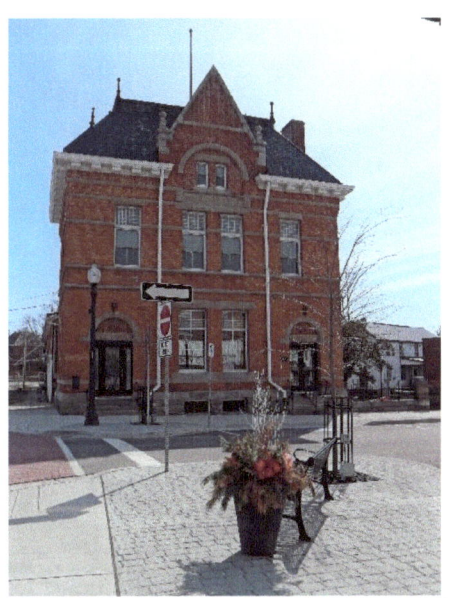

12 Cayuga Street North – Post Office

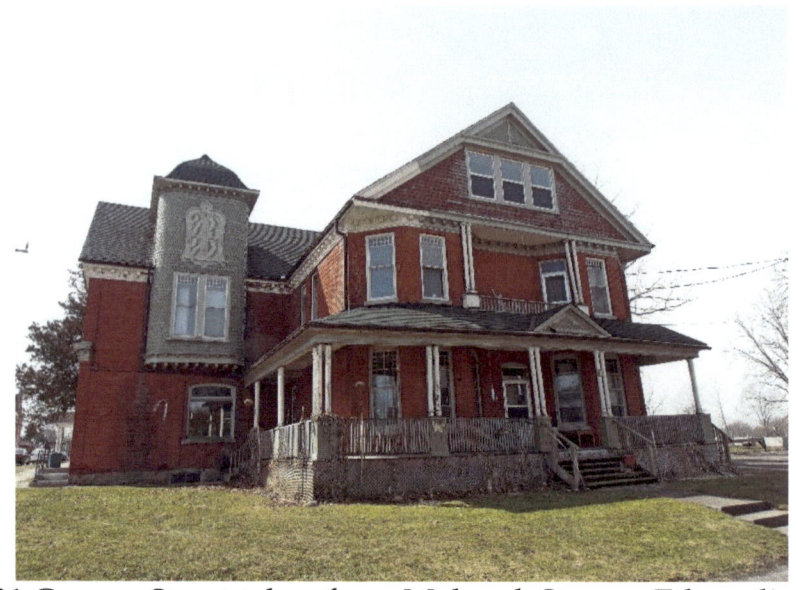

31 Cayuga Street taken from Mohawk Street – Edwardian with bay windows, turret in wing

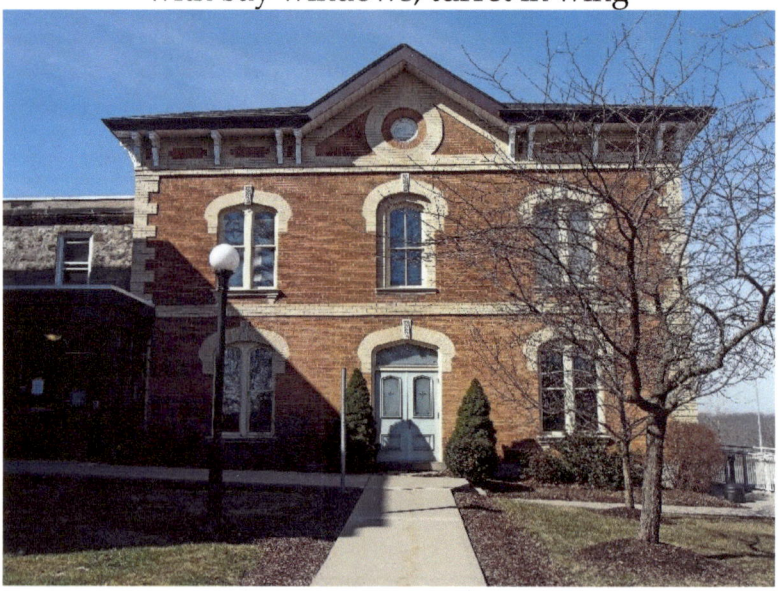

55 Munsee Street – Jailer's Residence – 1877 – Italianate style, low hipped roof, overhanging eaves with brackets, a bullseye window

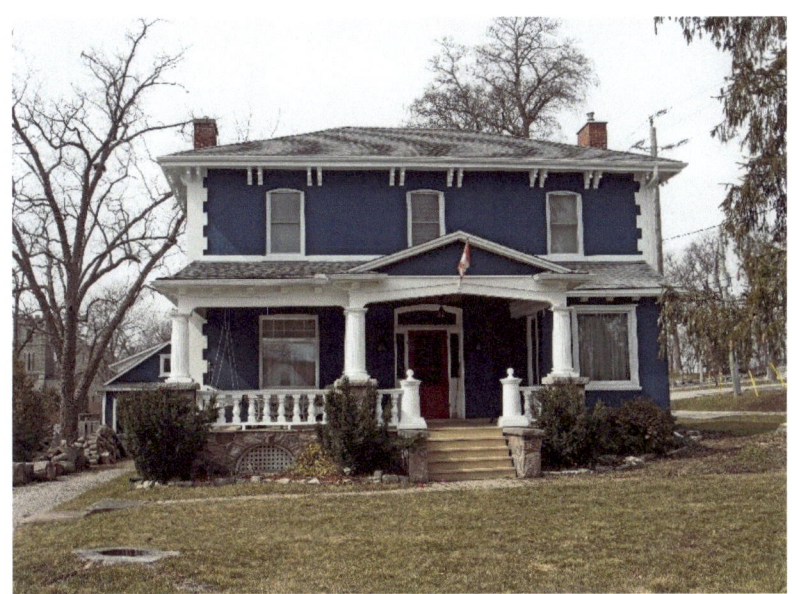

Munsee Street – Italianate, paired cornice brackets

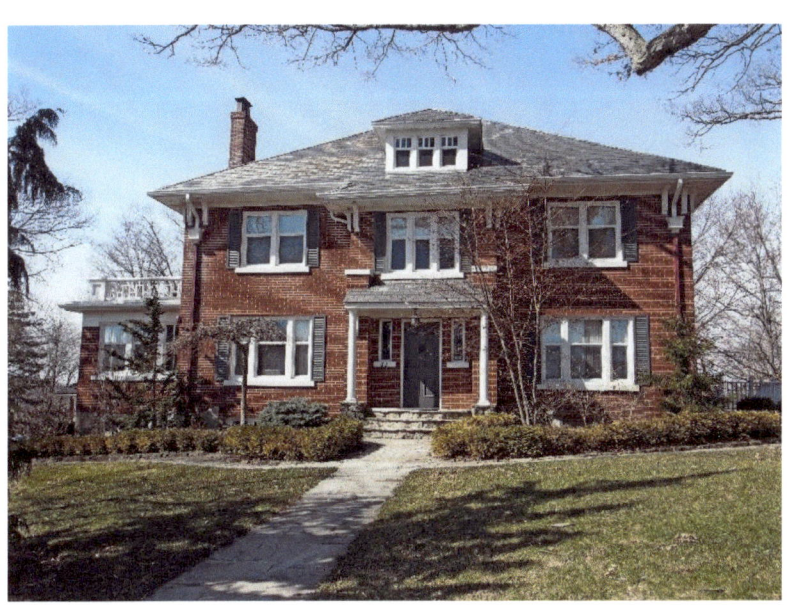

41 Echo Street – Italianate, dormer in attic

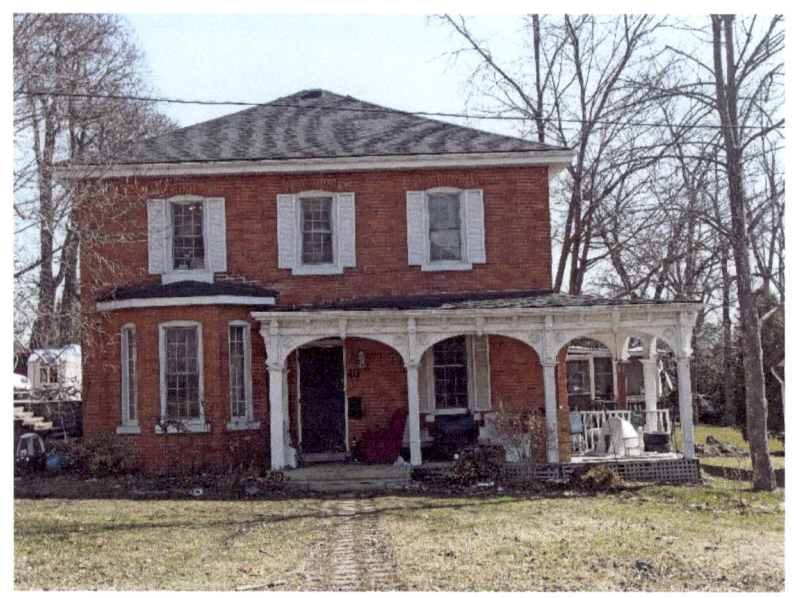
40 Ottawa Street – hipped roof, bay window

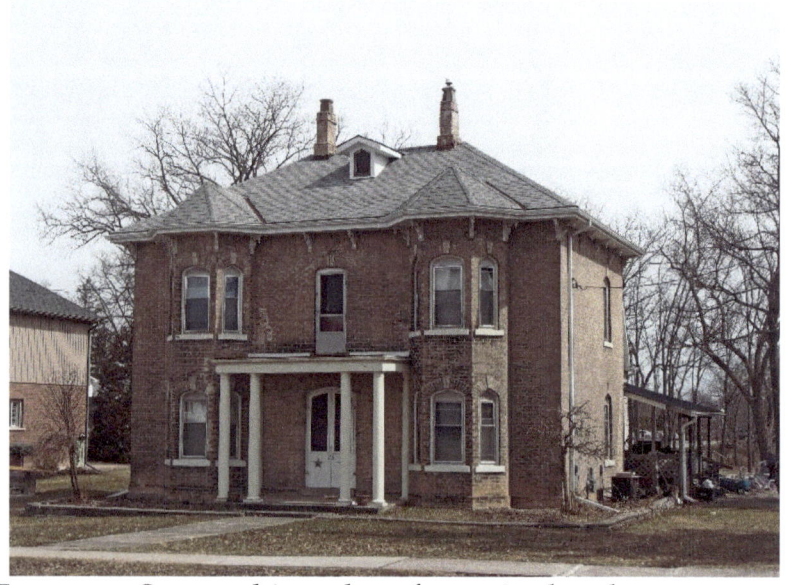
26 Tuscarora Street – hipped roof, cornice brackets, two-story bay windows

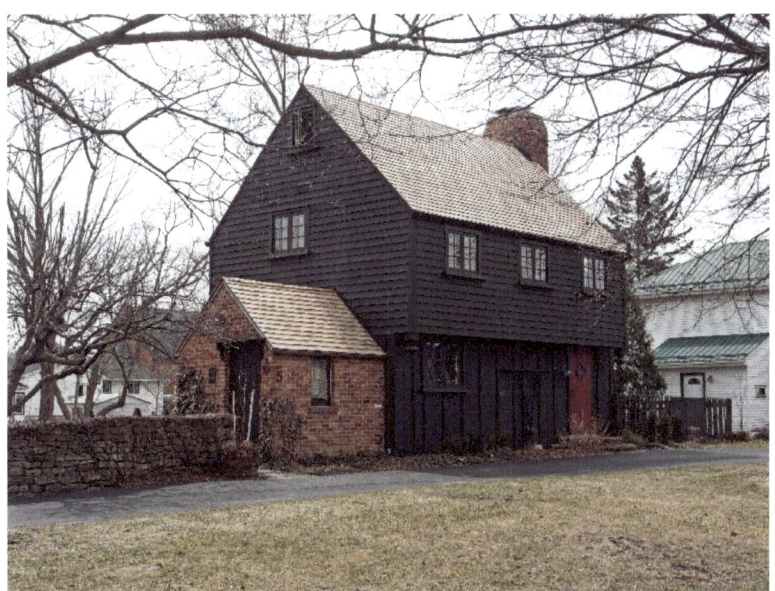

5 Mohawk Street – The Duff House - replica of a 17th century New England Garrison style house – steep pitched cedar-shake A-roof, second storey overhang, double casement wooden windows

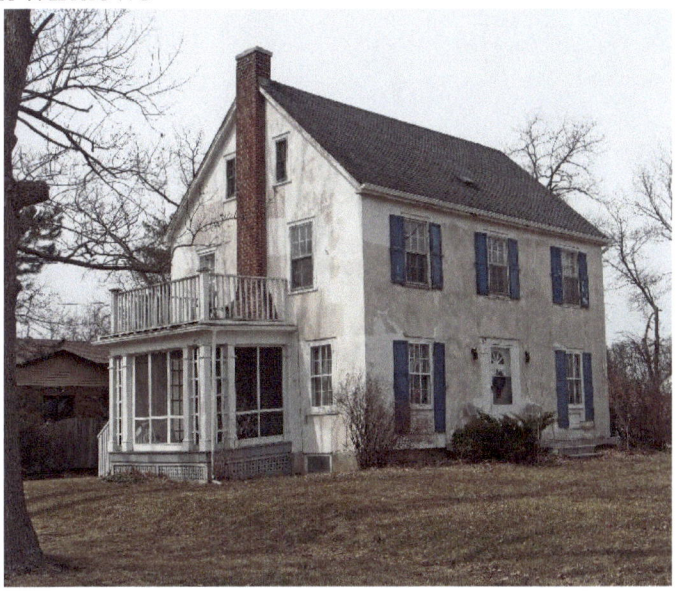

17 Winnett Street – gable roof, balanced façade

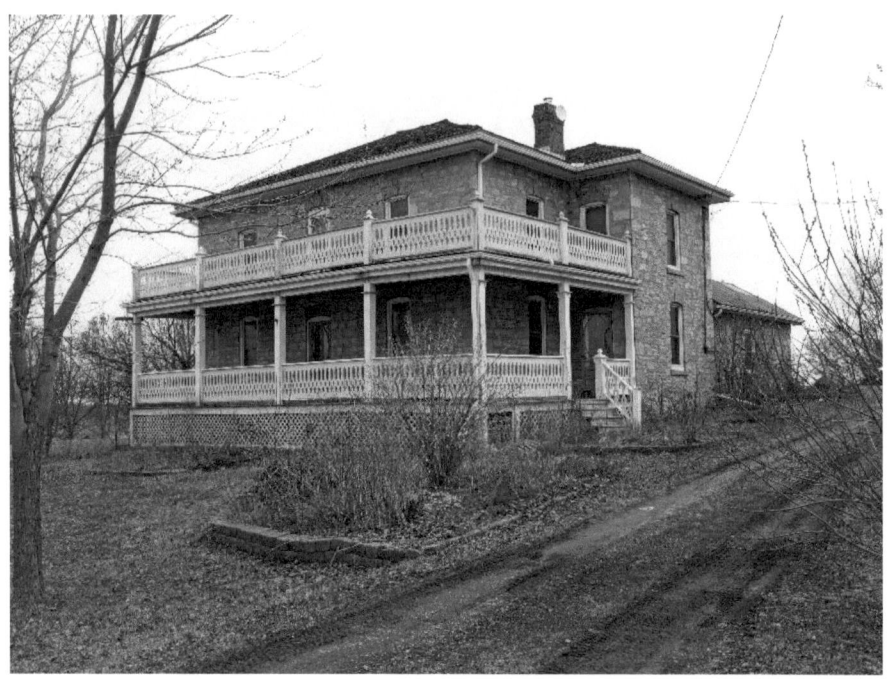

4104 Highway 3 – Campbell-Pine House – c. 1895 – limestone farmhouse with hipped roof, two-storey veranda; a large portion of Donald Campbell's 1847 stone cottage is incorporated into the walls of the house. Donald Campbell was one of the earliest settlers of North Cayuga Township; he operated a steam sawmill on the premises.

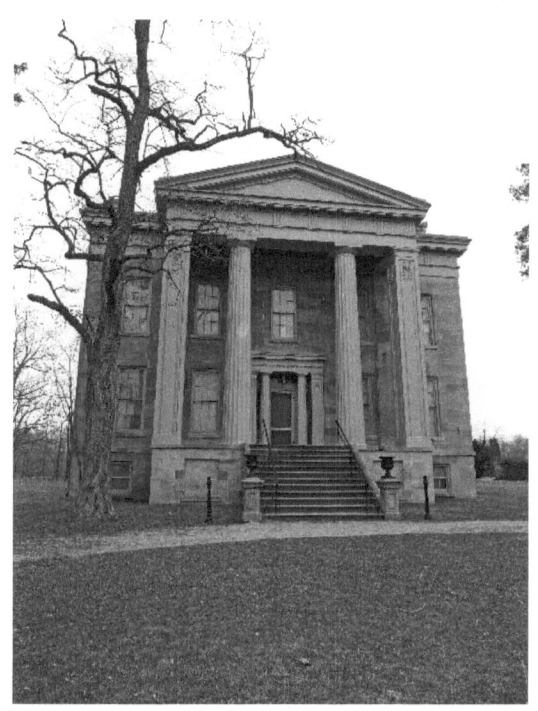

243 Haldimand Highway 54 - Ruthven Estate, the main house and wing, c. 1845, was designed by the master building/architect John Latshaw. Ruthven Park is a 1,500-acre country estate. The house is in the Greek Revival style with a broad staircase leading to a front landing with classical columns. The south wing was added c. 1860, the south-east wing c. 1880, and the east wing c. 1884. It was the former home of five generations of the Thompson family from the 1840s to 1990s. David Thompson came to the area and started a saw mill in 1834, and added a grist mill in 1836. David was instrumental in the laying out of the former 1200-acre town of Indiana. He eventually owned two sawmills, as well as a gristmill, carding mill, cooperage, and several stores. Overall, Indiana supported over thirty industries and was the largest industrial town in Haldimand County in the mid-nineteenth century.

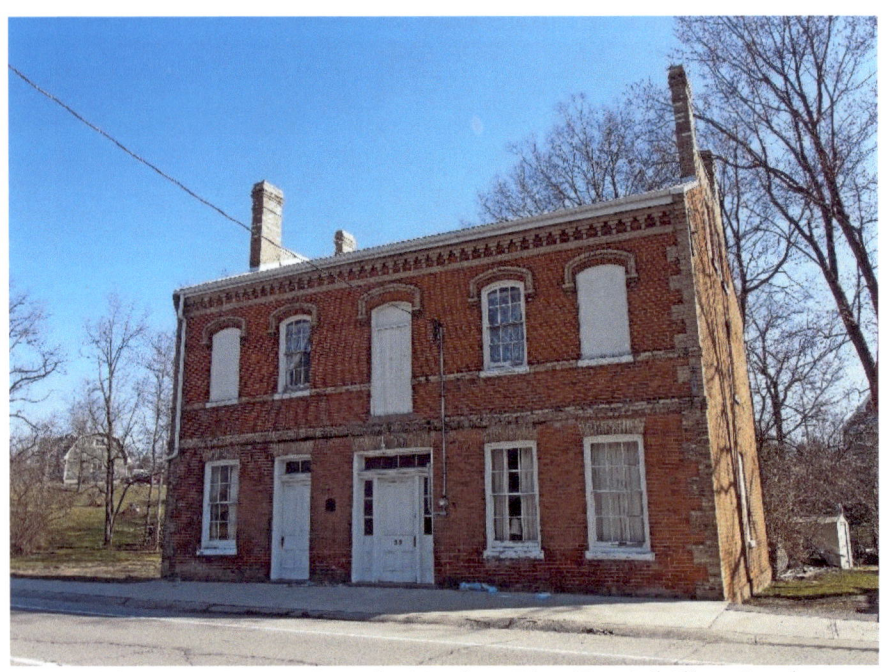

39 Front Street South, York – The Enniskillen Lodge, formerly the Barber Hotel, was built in 1862 for Mr. Daniel Barber, a prominent local hotelier. Large Georgian style windows, doors, and brick detailing are spaced and designed symmetrically. It has a projected cornice with dentils, Regency four-panel door with sidelights and rectangular transom, hood molds over windows, horizontal banding, and corner quoins.

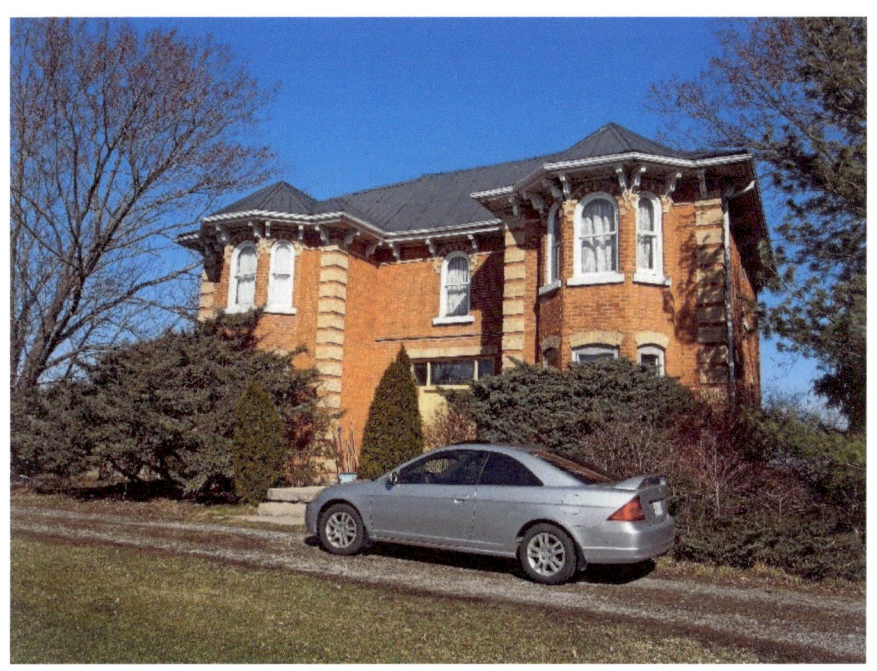

2389 Haldimand Road 9 – Italianate – cornice brackets, corner quoins, two-story bay windows

Dunnville, Ontario Book 1 in Colour Photos – My Top 11 Picks

Dunnville is a community near the mouth of Grand River in Haldimand County, and is only a few kilometers from Lake Erie. Dunnville was one of the early thriving centers of Upper Canada and Ontario. Following the American Revolution, a six-mile strip of land on both sides of the Grand River from its mouth to its sources was opened up to settlement by displaced members of the Six Nations Confederacy. The land was granted to the Iroquois tribes by the British to compensate the Confederacy for land lost in the United States during the revolution.

The British originally intended the land to remain in the hands of the Indians, but Mohawk Chief Joseph Brant wanted to open it up to settlement in order to create a source of revenue. Brant persuaded the Six Nations to surrender large blocks of land. Many of the early European arrivals were United Empire Loyalists.

By 1825, twenty-five people lived around Dunnville with a grist mill, a saw mill, and a distillery owned by Squire Anthony who was perhaps the first settler in the area. William Hamilton Merritt is called the Father of Canadian Transportation. With his vision and energy, the Feeder Canal connected Dunnville to the rest of the Welland Canal which flowed from Port Dalhousie on Lake Ontario to Welland. Large amounts of timber were shipped by scows from the Grand River to Buffalo and other markets for use as fuel for the new and growing railroads.

The initial Dunnville Dam was finished in 1829, in time for the opening of the Welland Canal in November of that year. The project brought laborers to the area, creating a need for farm produce and housing. The damming of the river provided a reliable source of power which supported mills and businesses including a tannery and a cloth factory. Dunnville was also served by the Buffalo, Brantford and Goderich Railway and was an important port which warranted its own government customs office.

By 1907, Dunnville had four large textile mills. Textiles continued to fuel the town's development for many years.

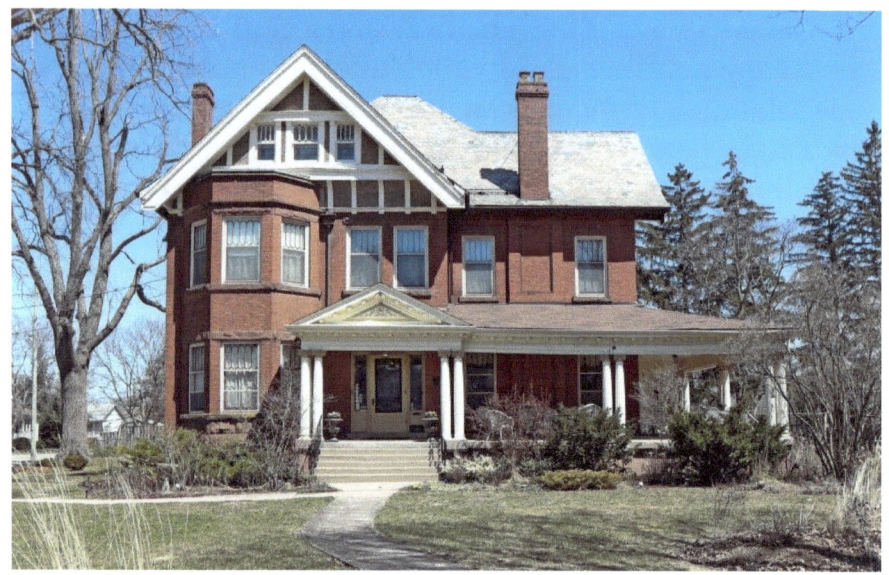

241 Broad Street West – The Lalor Estate is a two-and-a-half-storey residence with a four-gable roof and a wraparound veranda with fluted columns. This Edwardian structure was built in 1905. Its builder was Francis Ramsey Lalor, a prominent Dunnville businessman, politician, philanthropist, and entrepreneur. His business interests included two dry goods stores, a grocery store, an apple evaporator, natural gas wells, the F.R. Lalor Canning Factories, the F.R. Lalor Ashes Company, and the Monarch Knitting Mills. The exterior walls are red brick. There is a two-storey bay window, Tudor-style timbering in the gable, a pediment above the entrance with a decorative tympanum, and sidelights beside the front door.

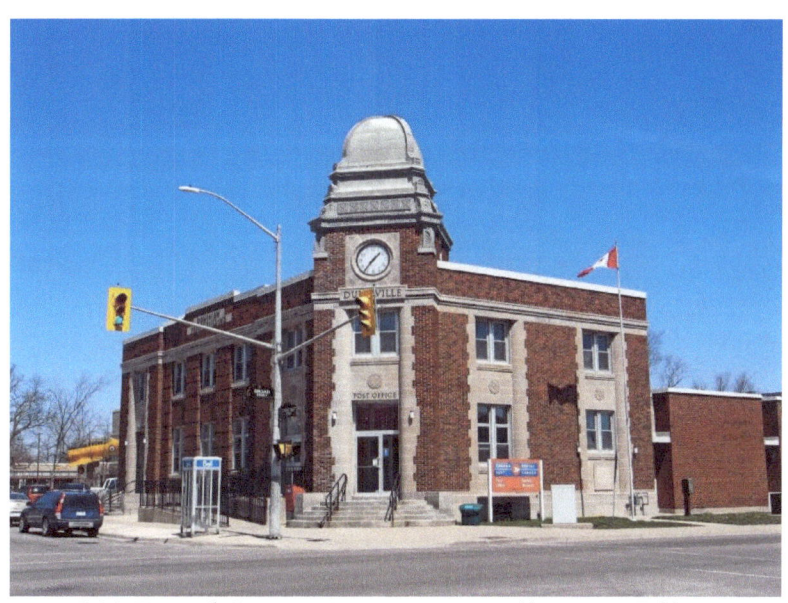

201 Broad Street East – Dunnville Post Office

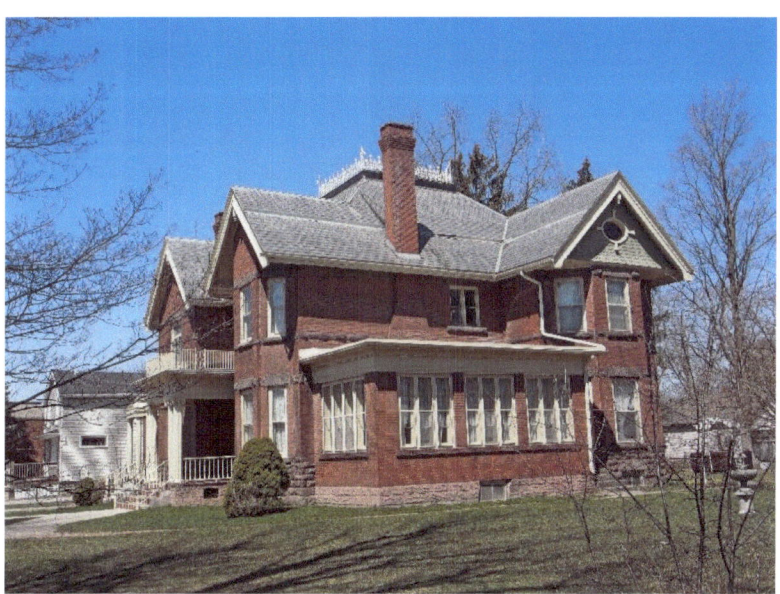

119 Broad Street East – widow's walk with iron cresting, dormer, Ionic pillars, circular window in side gable

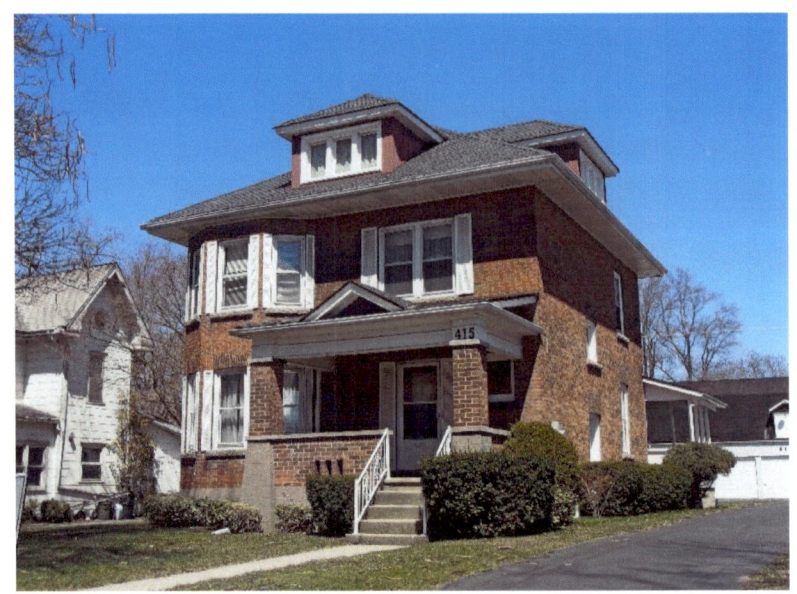

415 Niagara Street – dormers in hip roof, two-storey bay window

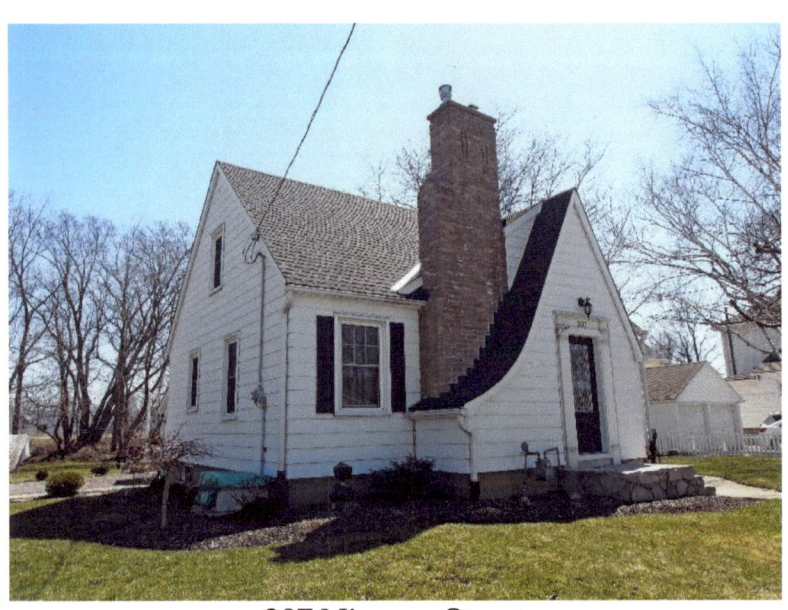

307 Niagara Street

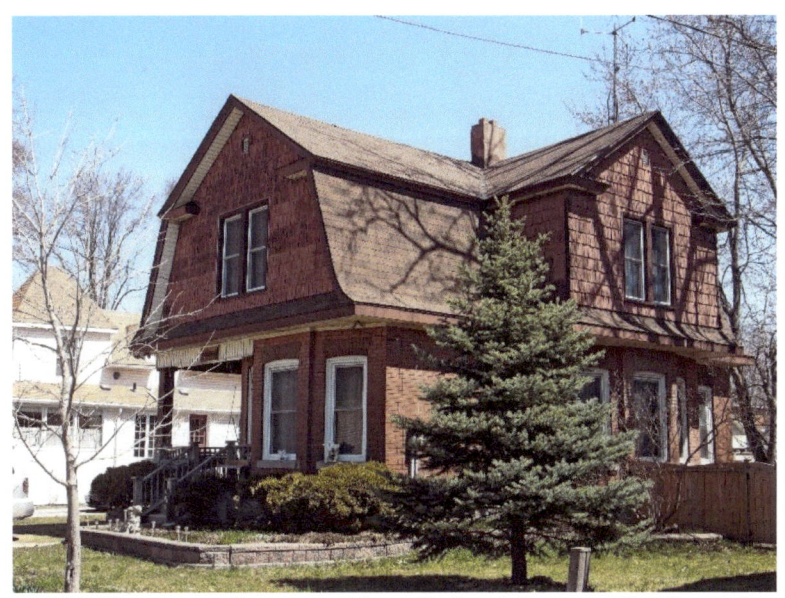

307 Tamarac Street – Neo-Colonial – gambrel roof

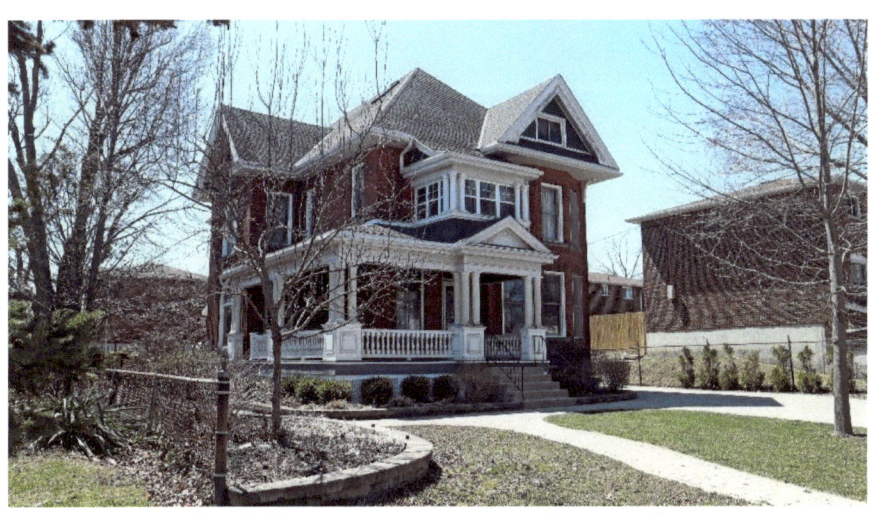

Lock Street – wraparound veranda

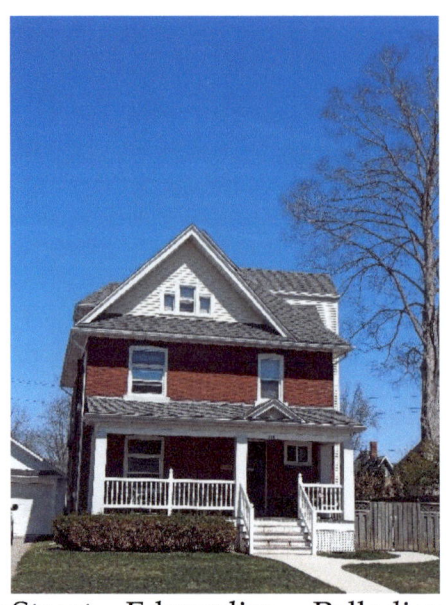

213 Lock Street – Edwardian – Palladian window

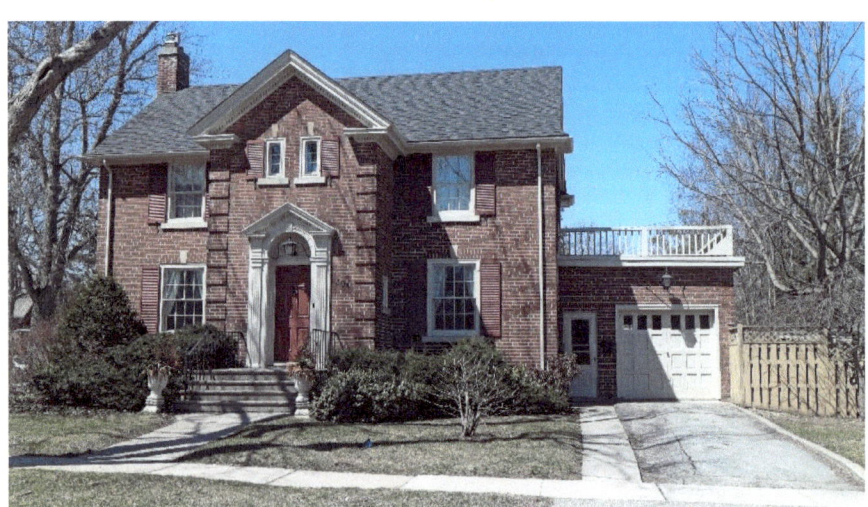

304 Church Street – two-storey frontispiece with quoins and cornice return on gable

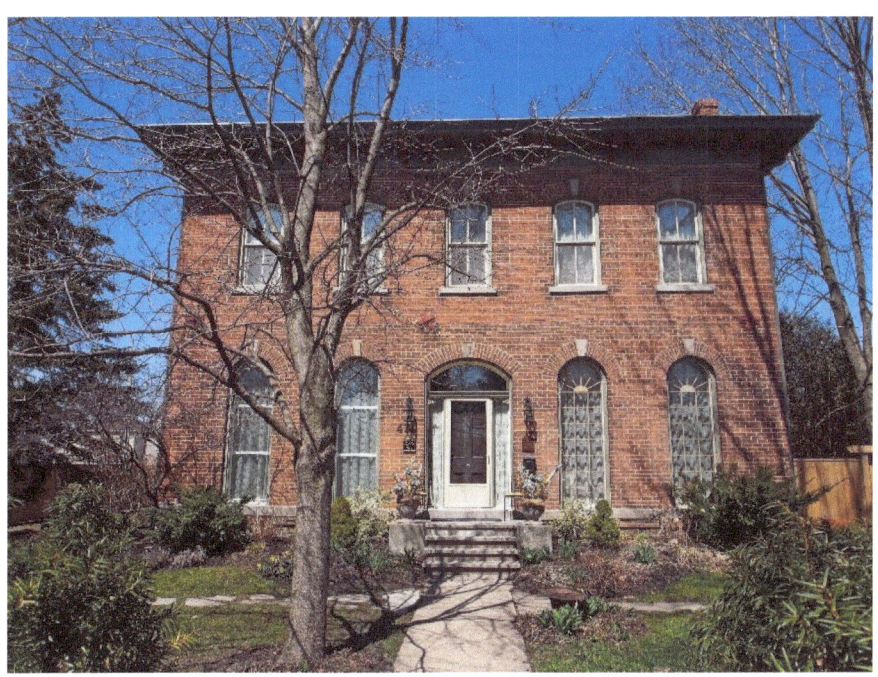

431 Queen Street – George Sime emigrated from Scotland to Canada in the 1840s and settled in Dunnville. He was a tanner and courier by trade; he was a respected businessman and prominent landowner involved in local politics. He built this two-storey home in 1869 in the Italianate style of architecture. The hipped roof has projecting eaves with paired cornice brackets. The keystone above the entrance has a thistle; there are sidelights and a transom surrounding the door. The middle keystone on the upper storey has the date.

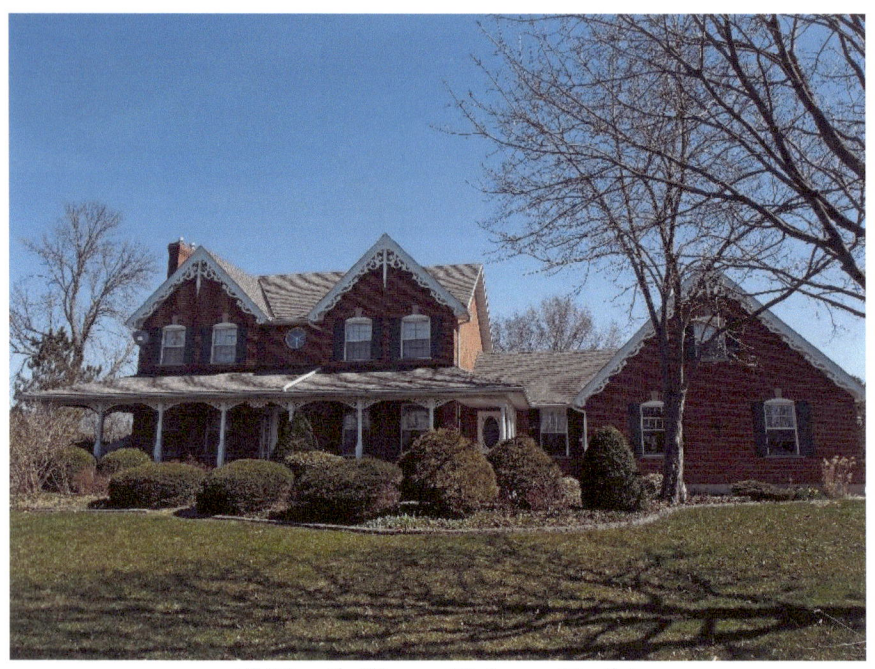

48 North Shore Drive - Gothic

Dunnville, Ontario Book 2 and Area in Colour Photos – My Top 16 Picks

Haldimand County is a municipality on the Niagara Peninsula in Southern Ontario, on the north shore of Lake Erie, and on the Grand River. Haldimand was first created as a county in 1800, from a portion of Norfolk. It was named after the governor of the Province of Quebec Sir Frederick Haldimand. From 1974 to 2000, Haldimand County and Norfolk County were merged to form the Regional Municipality of Haldimand-Norfolk.

The population centers in Haldimand are Caledonia, Dunnville, Hagersville, Jarvis and Cayuga. Most of Haldimand is agricultural land, although some heavy industry, including the Nanticoke Generating Station, is located here. Some of the smaller communities within the municipality are Byng, Canborough, Canfield, Cheapside, Fisherville, Kohler, Lowbanks, Nanticoke, Rainham Centre, Selkirk, South Cayuga, Sweets Corners, and York.

Dunnville is a community near the mouth of Grand River in Haldimand County, and is only a few kilometers from Lake Erie.

South Cayuga lies on the north shore of Lake Erie, ten kilometers east of Dunnville. Initially part of the Six Nations of the Grand River Indian Reserve, the heavy clay soil of South Cayuga Township was well suited to the cultivation of grain, hay, and livestock.

Sweet's Corners is located on Rainham Road west of South Cayuga.

Kohler was named for the Kohler family, one of many German immigrants who came to the area in the mid-1800s. It is located on County Road 8 south of Cayuga, and north of Rainham Centre.

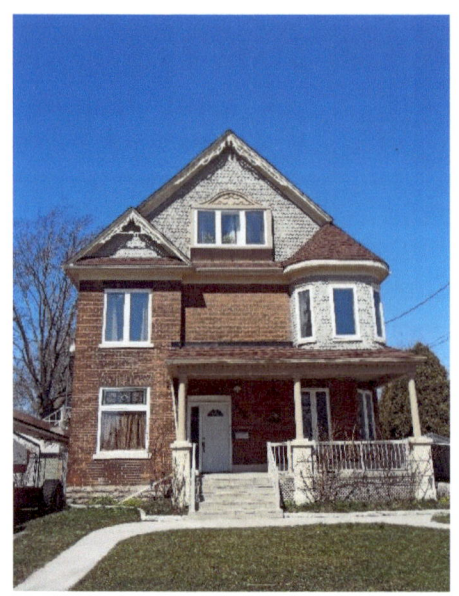

111 Alder Street - turret

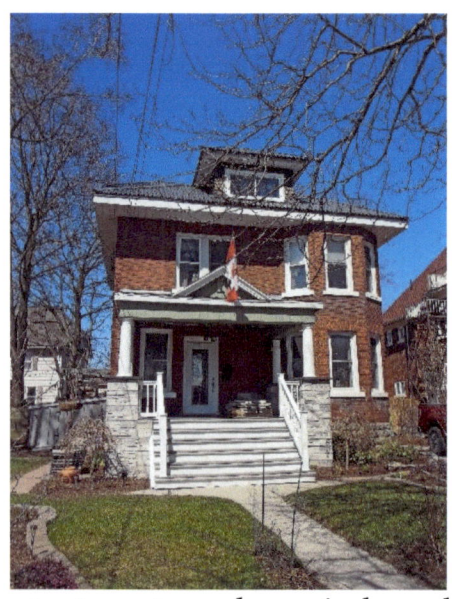

109 Alder Street – two-storey bay window, dormer in attic

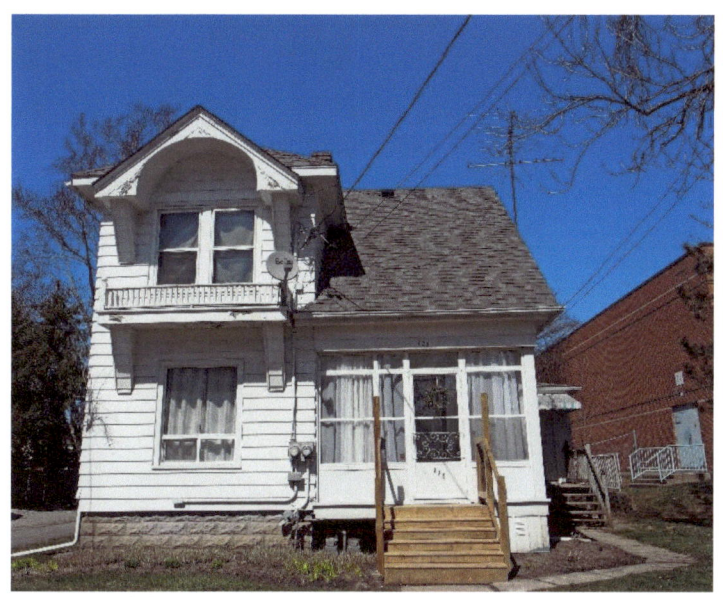

225 Alder Street West – second floor balcony

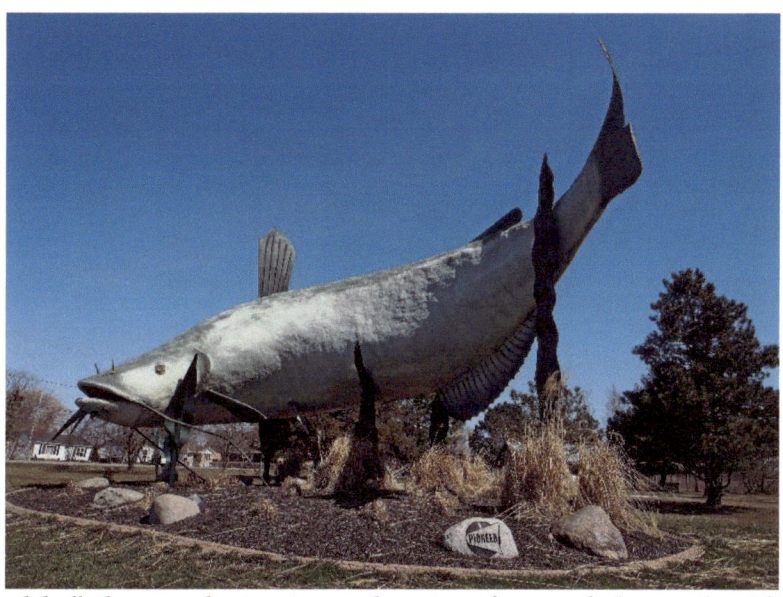

"Muddy" the mudcat - A mudcat is a form of channel catfish and has long been associated with Dunnville. At over fifty feet in length, this is the largest statue of its kind in the world.

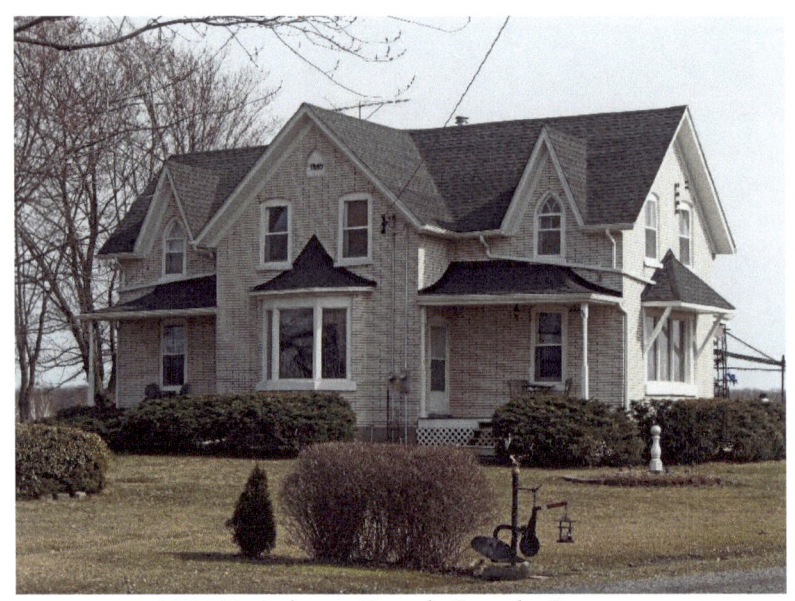
6156 Rainham Road, South Cayuga

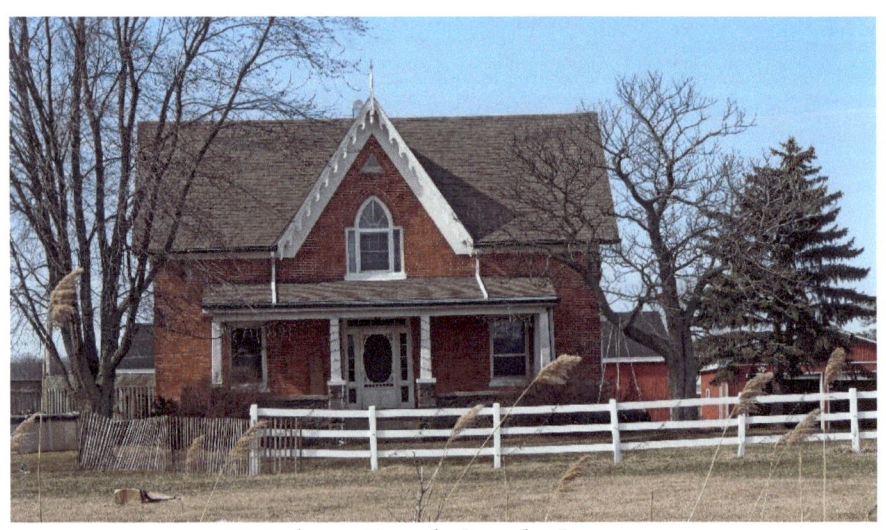
Rainham Road, South Cayuga

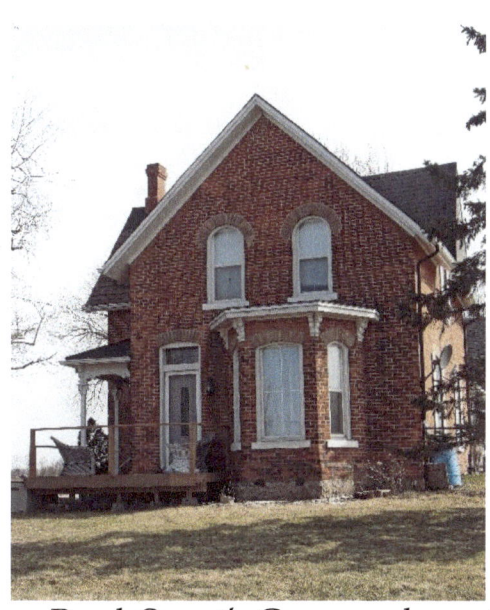

5330 Rainham Road, Sweet's Corners – bay window with cornice brackets

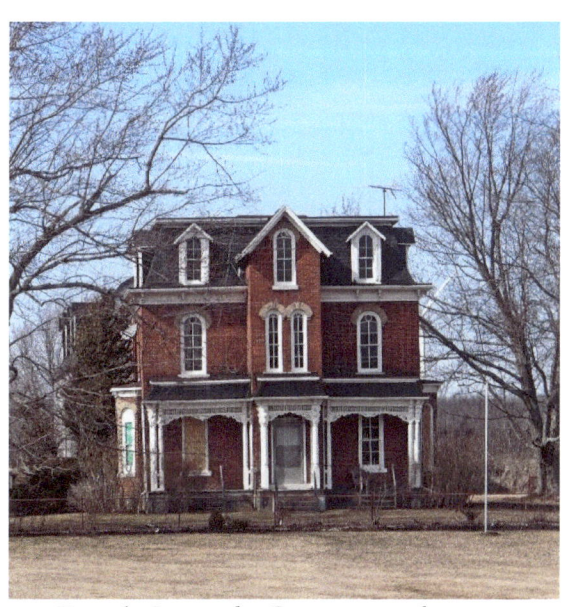

6027 Rainham Road, Sweet's Corners – three-storey, mansard roof, frontispiece, bay window on side, full-width veranda

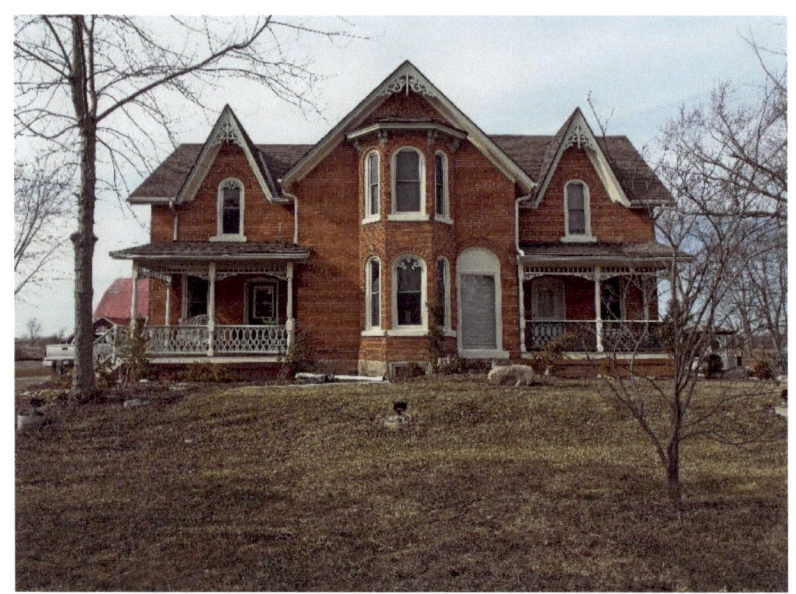

2191 Lakeshore Road – Gothic – two-storey baby window, verge board trim on gables

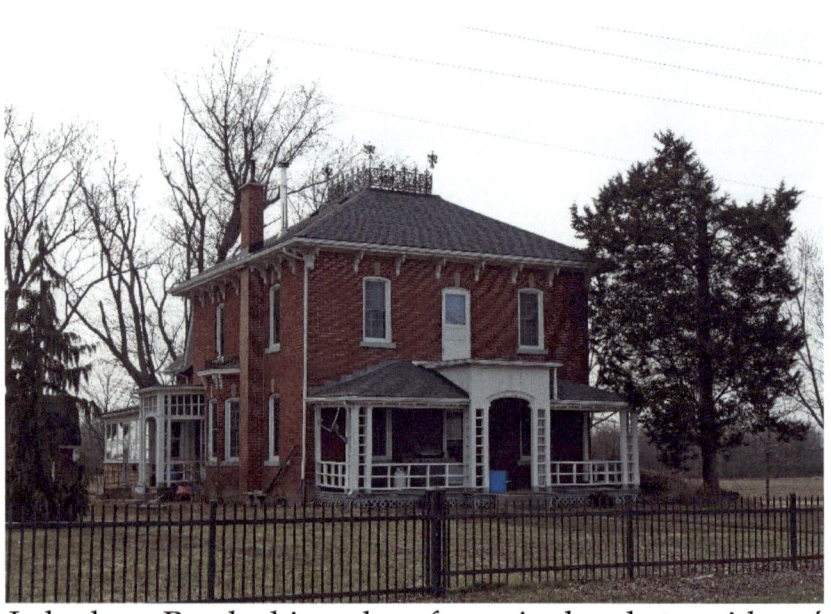

Lakeshore Road – hipped roof, cornice brackets, widows' walk on rooftop

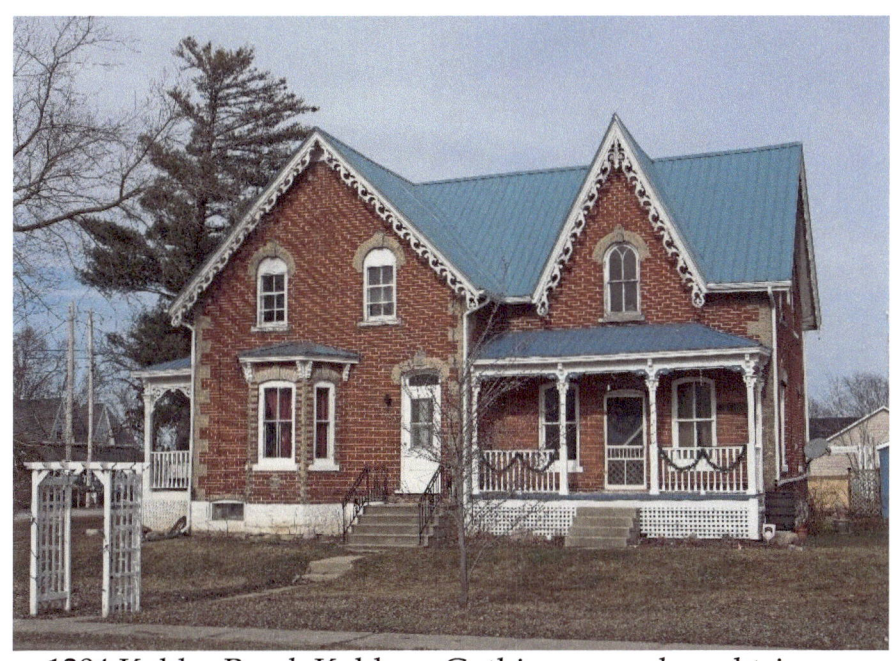

1204 Kohler Road, Kohler – Gothic – verge board trim on gables, bay window

Other Books by Barbara Raue

Coins of Gold
Arrows, Indians and Love
The Life and Times of Barbara
The Cromwell Family Book
Laura Secord Discovered
Daddy Where Are You?

Montana Series
Book 1: Montana Dream
Book 2: Life on the Montana Frontier
Book 3: Montana to Boston and Back
Book 4: Montana Sons Go to War
Book 5: Montana Sons Return from War

Book 1: Rite of Passage
Book 2: Rite of Marriage

© 2019 by Barbara Raue - All the photos in this book have been taken with my cameras. I own the rights to them.

Barbara is The Authority on Saving Our History One Photo at a Time. She is pursuing her interest in photography and architecture by preserving a record through photos of old buildings from the 1800s and 1900s with their unique architecture. Enjoy the beautiful architecture in the comfort of your living room. Dream about what it was like in those by-gone days. Dream about what it was like to live in a mansion like one of those in this book.

Barbara Raue, a wife, mother and grandmother, is an avid reader and writer. She has researched and compiled several family histories. In 2010, Barbara published her book "Coins of Gold," which celebrates the courageous life of her mother, May Todd. Barbara's second book is a historical fiction "Arrows, Indians and Love" which takes place in Boonesborough, Kentucky during the time of Daniel Boone. In 2013, Barbara published *The Cromwell Family Book* in which she traces her ancestry generations back into Great Britain. Her second novel is called *Laura Secord Discovered,* in which the story of Laura's service during the War of 1812 is shared. Barbara's memoir is titled *Daddy Where Are You?* It tells of her life growing up without a father. Five novels in the Montana Series have been published, *Montana Dream, Life on the Montana Frontier, Montana to Boston and Back, Montana Sons Go to War*, and *Montana Sons Return from War*.

This is a link to Barbara's website to view all of her books
http://barbararaue.ca

www.ingramcontent.com/pod-product-compliance
Lightning Source LLC
Chambersburg PA
CBHW040242220526
45473CB00001B/338